Tales and Legends
about Mathematical & Scientific Insights

Igor Ushakov

Enigmatic Terra Al-Jabr

San Diego
2012

Series

"Stories and Legends about Mathematical Insights"

Book 1. Man's first steps takes us through the first use of scientific and mathematical thinking as man began to question the nature of his Universe and then takes us into the history of measurements of the physical quantities of temperature, length, time and mass.

Book 2. In the beginning was the number … You find here new facts about Roman and Arabic numbers and some interesting methods of calculations. You also find here interesting things about magic numbers.

Book 3. The Magic of Geometry shows how the common problems of measuring land led to the development of mathematical discipline. You will know about unusual and impossible figures. You will have a pleasure to look at fantastic fractals.

Book 4. Enigmatic Terra Al-Jabr tells the stories of the origin and formation of algebra. You find from here that it is really interesting branch of mathematics.

Book 5. It's a Random, Random, Random World presents entertaining stories about the development of probability and statistics theory.

These books help teachers make their classes more interesting and help pupils to know even more than their teachers!

Cover design: Igor A. Ushakov.

To my beloved granddaughters
Anastasia & Alisa

Preface

The subject of mathematics is so serious that nobody should miss an opportunity to make it a little bit entertaining.

Blaise Pascal[1].

What is this book about? For whom is it written? Why is it written in this manner, not in another? Discussion about geometry, algebra and similar topics definitely hint that this is about mathematics. On the other hand, you cannot find within a proof of any statement or strong chronology of facts. Thus, this is not a tutorial book on mathematics or on of mathematics. This is just a collection of interesting and sometimes exciting stories and legends about human discoveries in one or another way connected to mathematics…

Our book is open for everybody who likes to enrich their intelligence with the stories of genius insights and great mistakes (mistakes also can be great!), and with biographies of creators of mathematical thinking and mathematical approaches in the study of the World.

Who are the readers of the proposed book? We believe that there is no special audience in the sense of education or age. The books could be interesting to schoolteachers and university professors (not necessarily mathematicians!) who would like to make their lectures more vivid and intriguing. At the same time, students of different educational levels as well as their parents may find here many interesting facts and ideas. We can imagine that the book could be interesting even for state leaders whose educational level is enough to read something beyond speeches prepared for them by their advisors.

Trust us: we tried to write the book clearly! Actually, it is non-mathematical book around mathematics.

This book is not intended to convert you to a "mathematical religion". Indeed, there is no need to do this: imagine how boring life would be if everybody were a mathematician? Mathematics is the world of

---

[1] **Blaise Pascal** (1623 –1662), was a French mathematician, physicist, inventor, writer and philosopher.

ideas, however any idea needs to be realized: integrals cannot appease your hunger, differential equations cannot fill gas tank of your car....

However, to be honest, we pursued the objective: we tried to convince you, the reader, that without mathematics *homo erectus* would never transform into *homo sapiens.*

Now, let us travel into the very interesting place: Terra Mathematica. We'll try to make this your trip interesting and exciting.

Igor Ushakov

Contents

1. From Arithmetics to Algebra

It has been said that the human mind has never invented a labor-saving machine equal to algebra.
Josiah Gibbs [2]

1.1. From counting to calculations

What science else is more honorable, more admirable, more useful for manhood than mathematics?
Benjamin Franklin [3]

The simplest mathematical concept is a number. One, who is dealing with numbers, needs some actions with it: summation, extraction, and then multiplication and dividing… Of course, you observed as a small child begins to possess first understanding of summation.

The number and calculations appeared many thousands years ago. In this connection, probably, it is the appropriate time to remember about ontogenesis[4] and phylogenies[5]:

---

[2] **Josiah Willard Gibbs** (1839 - 1903) was an outstanding American mathematical-engineer, theoretical physicist, and chemist. He was an inventor of vector analysis. He spent his entire career at Yale, which awarded him the first American Ph.D. in engineering in 1863.

[3] **Benjamin Franklin** (1706-1790)was one of the most important Founding Fathers of the United States. He was a leading author, political theorist, politician, printer, scientist, inventor, civic activist, and diplomat.

[4] **Ontogenesis**, or morphogenesis describes the origin and the development of an organism from the fertilized egg to its mature form.

[5] Philogenesis describes a historical development of a population of various organisms.

development of an individual (fertilization of an egg, birth, growth, aging and death) reflects in development of entire population. Among humorous biologist a following joke exists: a million years is a period of time needed to transform an ape into a Ph.D.

And in the same way as development of a child in a modern family differs from development of Kipling's Mawgli[6], people of civilized society differ from tribesmen of isolated group. For instance, in XIX century in Amazon River area scientists discovered an Indian tribe where people counted only from 1 to 3. The larger numbers were considered unaccountably large like Greeks' "myriad".

However, with development of arithmetic people needed more precise mathematical methods. It was the time when algebra enters the scene of mathematical theater.

Algebra originated at antediluvian times. It is known that about 4 millenniums ago, Sumerians could solve quadratic equations and solved systems of two linear equations (and one of them could be even quadratic!). Those equations describe various practical problems related to measurement of land plots. Of course, it is needed to mention that there were no equations in a form we used to deal with now: it was verbal descriptions. The very first notations for unknown quantities were introduced only by ancient Greek mathematician Diophant (II century B.C.).

---

[6] **Mowgli** is a personage of a fairytale "The Jungle Book" written by English writer and poet Joseph Rudyard Kipling (1865-1936). Mawgli was found and adapted by she-wolf and grew in jungles. He appeared in a human society when he already was a teenager.

1.2. The Oldest Mathematical Problem

First one arises to axioms and afterwards descents to practice.

Francis Bacon [7]

In Rhind's papyrus[8], dated about II millennium B.C., there is, evidently, the first algebraic problem ever. It contains the following: Five people shared 100 breads. The second one got as much as the first one and some additional portion. The third one got as much as the second one and the same additional portion. Same repeats with others: the next one got as much as previous plus the same additional portion as previous. At the same time it is known that the first and the second together got as much as one seventh of what the three remaining got. How many breads everyone has got?

It is clear just from the problem formulation that the fifth of them was the most successful: he got more than anybody. However, it is interesting how much unjust was that sharing of breads?

Let us denote the part of the first participant of that sharing by x, and difference between two neighbors numbers (that additional portion) denote by y. Thus, all 100 breads are divided in the following way:

$$x + (x + y) + (x + 2y) + (x + 3y) + (x + 4y) = 100.$$

Now let us use an additional condition:

$$7[x + (x + y)] = (x + 2y) + (x + 3y) + (x + 4y).$$

---

[7] **Francis Bacon** (1561-1626) was an English philosopher, statesman, and essayist

[8] **Rhind's papyrus** is called after the name of its owner – British Egyptologist Alexander Henry Rhind (1833 – 1863). This papyrus is also called London papyrus due to its location in the British Museum. That papyrus is one of the oldest one with mathematical contents.

So, we have a system of two linear equations with two unknown quantities. After obvious simplifications we could re-write the system in the form that is more usual for us:

$$\begin{cases} x + 2y = 20 \\ 11x = 2y, \end{cases}$$

and one easily finds $x = 1\frac{2}{3}$ and $y = 9\frac{1}{6}$. So, the sharing led to the following: the first one got a bread and two third of a bread, the second one– 10 and 5/6, the third one – 20, the forth one – 29 and 1/6, and the fifth one – 38 и 1/3! (More than unjust sharing...)

Of course, this problem is simple for us. However, how it was solved by ancient Egyptians?

1.3. Diophantus and Diophantine Equations

Unsophisticated puzzles with integers through centuries were a source of renewing of mathematics.

George Birhgof[9]

We know almost nothing about Diophantus' life. There is a legend that he left his "autobiography" as a "mathematical epitaph" inscribed on his tomb.

> "This tomb holds Diophantus. Ah, what a marvel!
> And the tomb tells scientifically the measure of his life.
> God vouchsafed that he should be a boy for the sixth part of his life;
> When a twelfth was added, his cheeks acquired a beard;

[9] **George David Birkhoff** (1884-1944) was an American mathematician, one of the most important leaders in American mathematics in his generation.

He kindled for him the light of marriage after a seventh,
And in the fifth year after his marriage He granted him a son.
Alas! Late-begotten and miserable child,
When he had reached the measure of half his father's life,
The chill grave took him.
After consoling his grief by this science of numbers for four years,
He reached the end of his life."

Diophantus of Alexandria

(between A.D. 200 and 214 to 284 or 298)

Ancient Greek mathematician from Alexandria who was called in Medieval time as "the Father of Algebra". He is the author of a series of classical mathematical books called "*Arithmetica*" in 13 volumes, of which only first six survived. He also wrote a manuscript about the so-called polygonal numbers. He worked with equations which we now call Diophantine equations. He was the first who introduced letter notation in algebra.

First Time his works were published in Europe in 1575 (in Latin).

This above mathematical problem can be reduced to a linear equation. So, let us solve it. Let us denote the length of Diophantus' life by x. From the text of the epitaph follows that $\frac{x}{6}$ of it took his childhood; $\frac{x}{12}$ took his youth; $\frac{x}{7}$ passed before he married and in 5 years his son was born. The son has lived a half of the life of his father, i.e. $\frac{x}{2}$; next 4 years Diophantus mourned his son's death and died. Thus the total length of the Diophantus' life x can be written as the following sum:

$$\frac{x}{6}+\frac{x}{12}+\frac{x}{7}+5+\frac{x}{2}+4=x,$$

that might be re-written as

$$\left(1-\frac{1}{6}+\frac{1}{12}+\frac{1}{7}+\frac{1}{2}\right)x=9,$$

from where we get $x = 84$, i.e. Diophantus died at age 84.

Diophantus developed a very special mathematics – the so-called Diophantine equations, which do not differs from everybody knows, though there is an indispensable condition: the solutions have to be integers.

My son never heard about Diophantus of Diophantine equations nevertheless having an enter exam to an "elite" school, he gave a Diophantine solution of the problem he was asked.

An examiner asked him:

- What one gets if three chickens will be divided into two parts?

My son thought a bit and asked.

- Are those chicks alive or boiled?

The teacher almost jumped with her indignation:

- What's the difference?!

- If they are alive then in one part there will be two chicks and in another – one... However, if they are boiled than each part will have a chick and a half...

Ancient Greeks did not know negative numbers, so an equation of type

$$3x + 6 = 2x+1,$$

with solution $x = -5$, Diophantus called "inappropriate".

Among Diophantus' works the most important is "*Arithmetica*", which consists of 13 volumes.

After Diophantus' death, the Dark Ages began, spreading a shadow on math and science, and causing knowledge of Diophantus and the "*Arithmetica*" to be lost in Europe for about 1500 years. Six volumes were discovered by Regiomontanus[10] in Venice in 1463. Just recently the Arabic translation of four more Diophantus' books has been found. Unfortunately, there is practically no hope to find remaining three books…

DIOPHANTI
ALEXANDRINI
ARITHMETICORVM
LIBRI SEX.
ET DE NVMERIS MVLTANGVLIS
LIBER VNVS.

LVTETIAE PARISIORVM,
Sumptibus SEBASTIANI CRAMOISY, via
Iacobæa, sub Ciconiis.
M. DC. XXI.
CVM PRIVILEGIO REGIS.

In the first six saved Diophantus' books there are 189 problems accompanied with solutions. The first book contains common problems that lead to equation of the first and second orders. Remaining five volumes are dedicated to "indefinite", or Diophantine equations. Methods of their solution change from problem to problem, however namely this approach is considered as the greatest Diophantus input in mathematics.

Composing equations, Diophantus capably chose variables to make the problem most "transparent". For instance, one of his problemc is formulated as follows: "Find two numbers, the sum of which equals 20 and the product equals 96".

His solution is close to the following. The numbers are not equal otherwise each of them will be equals 10, so the product will be 100.

[10] **Johannes Regiomontanus** (1436 - 1476) was a German astronomer who designed first astronomical daily tables of planets location for 1475-1506 years, which were used by Vasko da Gama and Columbus. The author of the first work on trigonometry where problems of triangles construction were solved by algebraic methods rather than geometrical. The main work of Regiomontanus was translation of Ptolemy's "Almagest".

These numbers are symmetrical relatively to 10, i.e. one of them larger than 10, and another is smaller. So, these numbers might be written in the form $(10+x)$ and $(10-x)$. That leads us to equation

$$(10+x)(10-x)=96,$$

which, in turn, is equivalent to equation $x^2 = 4$. So, $x = 2$. (As we already mentioned at Ancient time people did not accept negative numbers.) Finally, solution is: numbers 8 and 12.

Here is another Diophantus' problem: "What is a minimum set of weights for weighing any load from 1 to 40 talents[11]?"

It is worth to note that Diophantus was the first who wrote a pure book of problems mostly with no solutions. In particular, this problem was given also with no solution. By all means, the Diophantus' solution was to have six weights: 1, 2, 4, 8, 16 and 32 talents. Indeed, such a set of weights allow weighing any load from 1 to 40 units:
$1 = 1$; $2 = 2$; $3 = 2 + 1$; $4 = 4$; $5 = 4 + 1$; and so on. Finally, $40 = 32 + 8$.

A witty solution of this problem was found by Gaspar Bachet[12], though ... almost two millenniums later! Bachet showed that for solving the problem there is enough only four weights 1, 3, 9 and 27 talents if it is permitted to put weight on both scales. Indeed,

$$1 = 1;\ 2 = 3-1;\ 3 = 3;\ 4 = 3+1;\ 5 = 9-3-1$$

... and, finally,

$$40 = 27 + 9 + 3 + 1.$$

Diophantus was on the threshold of introducing letter notations in algebra, he was the first one who used not only abbreviations but even symbols.

Unknown number he called in Greek *aritmos* (αριθμος in Greek means *number*). A unit he denoted by symbol ***μο*** and called *monas* (μονας means "one", or "single"). For the second power he introduces a symbol ***δν*** and called it *dunamis* (this Greek word has several meaning and one of

[11] A talent (Latin: talentum, from Ancient Greek: talanton which means "scale, balance") is an ancient unit of weight.

[12] **Clod Gaspar Bachet de Meziriak** (1581 - 1638)was a French mathematician and poet. In his book "Problèmes plaisants " (*Pleasanr Problems*) he presented a collection of ancient and other old problems. He translated and published Diophantus' "*Arithmetic*" into Latin and supplied the book with additions and comments.

them means *power*). The third power Diophantus denoted *κυ* and called *kubos* (*cube*). Larger powers forms with the use of composition like *dunamodunamis* for the 4th power, *dunamokubos* for the 5th power, *kuboskubos* for the 6th power. For these values he used first letters of corresponding words (*ar, du, ku, ddu, dku, kku*). Known numbers were supplied with a symbol ***μο***. Diophantus did not use a special symbol for summation> it was assumed that numbers following each other are summed. For extraction he used a symbol $\uparrow$, and equality was denoted by symbol *ις* (first letters of Greek word *isos* that means *equal*).

It was the beginning of algebra...

1.4. How equations were solved

> Algebra is generous. Very often it gives us more than we request.
>
> ***Jean D'Alembert***[13]

In China 2 millenniums B.C. people could solve equations of the first and second power and systems of linear equations. In the end of XIII century Chinese already knew binomial coefficients that are known us as "Pascal's Triangle". (In Europe this became known 250 years later.)

Indian mathematicians broadly used abbreviated notations for unknown quantities; they used irrational and negative numbers and were first who used zero not only for marking an "empty position" but as a quantity.

A real flourish of algebra was observed in Central Asia, in first turn, in Uzbekistan and Tajikistan. Algebra became an independent mathematical discipline.

The founder of algebra is believed to be al-Khorezmi that means "originally from Khorezm[14]" (calling also *Khwarazm*), the Middle Asia region where he was born).

[13] **Jean le Rond d'Alembert** (1717-1783) was a French mathematician, mechanic, physicist, and philosopher.

[14] Presently it is Khiva, a city in Uzbekistan.

Al-Khorezmi
(786-850)

Full name of the scientist sounds as Abu Ja'far Musa Ibn Musa al-Khorezmi, or al-Khawarizmi. Arabian mathematician, astronomer, astrologer, and geographer. A few is known about his life. It is known that he was one of the main scientists at the Palace of Wisdom in Baghdad.

He wrote the first textbook on arithmetic, some tractates on algebra and calendar. In his tractate on algebra there is a chapter on geometry, trigonometric tables and geographical coordinates main cities of the time.

He wrote in IX century a book titled "*The Compendious Book on Calculation by Completion and Balancing*", which was dedicated to solution of linear and quadratic equations. The title of the book sounded in Arabic like "*al-Kitab al-mukhtasar fi hisab al-jabr wa'l-muqabala*". The words "al-jabr" was laid in the name of the new branch of mathematics – *algebra*[15].

The term "completion" al-Khorezmi used for transferring subtrahend to the opposite side of equality and the term "balancing" meant transferring all known quantities in one side and all unknown quantities in other side.

He also wrote a tractate on Indian calculations the text of which is lost. There is only Latin translation "*Algoritmi de numero Indorum*", that is the title begins with distorted name of the author. Later the word "algoritmi" transforms into well-known "algorithm".

Al-Khorezmi and other scientists of Central Asia widely used algebra for accounting and similar purposes. Neither al-Khorezmi, nor his contemporaries did not use compact notations (abbreviations), since

[15] Translations of Arabic manuscripts into Latin that was the main scientific language in Medieval Europe led to such strange titles. It is time to remember a history with translation of "Almagest" by Claudius Ptolemy.

Arabic language is very compact: many words could be written with the use of a single symbol.

Notice that Arabian mathematicians did not accept Indian negative numbers and due to this they distinguished three particular types of quadratic equations: $x^2+px=q$, $x^2+q=p$ and $x^2=px+q$, where p and q are assumed positive.

Persian and Arabic mathematician of Central Asia enriched algebra with many new developments. In particular, for equations of higher powers they were able to find approximate solutions with an extreme accuracy. For instance, famous Persian scientist al-Biruni (who was, by the way, also born in Khorezm) reduced the problem of construction of 9-vertices polygon to solving a cubical equation $x^3=1+3x$ and found (in form of fractions with the 60-based numbers) the approximation

$$x=1,52'45''47'''13''''.$$

Abu Rayhan Muhammad ibn Ahmad al-Biruni

(973-1048)

He was a Persian mathematic-cian, physicist, philosopher, astrono-mer, astrologer, historian, anthro-pologist, geodesist, geologist, pharmacist, and teacher.

He wrote over 40 scientific works in Arabic. He found the Earth diameter and angle between ecliptic and the Equator.

Biruni has been described as "the first anthropologist" and the "father of geodesy".

For more details, see Chapter "Pantheon".

In modern form this approximation can be written as:

$$x = 1+\frac{52}{60}+\frac{45}{60^2}+\frac{47}{60^3}+\frac{13}{60^4}.$$

This value in decimal fractions gives accuracy up to the seventh decimal!

Classic poet and outstanding scientist Omar Khayyam, who wrote in Farsi[16], investigated in detail methods of solving cubical equations. Neither he, nor other mathematicians of the Muslim world could express the solution through coefficients of the equation though Omar Khayyam developed geometrical method of the roots finding. (Notice that he was interested only positive roots.)

Omar Khayyam
(1048 - 1131)

Persian mathematician, astronomer, philosopher who made an outstanding input in algebra development.

For wide circle of readers he is mostly known for his rubaiyat.

For more details, see Chapter 3 "Pantheon".

The history of algebra development in Medieval Europe reminds an enigmatic mixture of a detective story and a knights' tournament. In Medieval Italy it was common to arrange competitions between mathematicians.

In the beginning of this story, Scipione del Ferro[17] has found a general solution of the cubic equation but kept it in secret because such "know-how" was very critical for winning at mathematical tournaments. Just before his death, he opened his secret to his pupil Fiore[18]. In 1535 Fiore, armed with the "secret weapon" of his teacher, challenged to a "mathematical duel" one of the prominent mathematicians of the time, Niccolo Tartaglia.

---

16 **Farsi** is the most popular language of Central Asia and official language of Iran.

17 **Scipione del Ferro** (1465–1526) was an Italian mathematician, Professor of the University of Bologna, who is famous for being the first to find a formula to solve a cubic equation.

18 **Antonio Mario Fiore** was a pupil of del Ferro who was known only due to his "word duel" with Niccolo Tartaglia.

Later, Tartaglia wrote: "I used all my abilities, studiousness and skill to find how to solve such equations, and I have found it ten days before the competition due to my lucky chance".

During the competition each competitor should solve 30 problems that were delivered by the opponent. Tartaglia had solved al Fiore's problems in two hours when Fiore could not solve a single one presented by Tartaglia!

After the victory, Tartaglia began to keep his method in secret...

Niccolo Fontana Tartaglia
(1500-1557)

Italian mathematician whose nickname means "stuttered". During occupation of Italy by France, when he was 12 years old, he was severely wounded in his jaw. It led to strong deformation of his speaking abilities. So, he got that nickname and used it instead of real name (Fontana).

Being an autodidact, he conceived mathematics and was very successful. He also was famous in mechanics, ballistics and topography.

At the next stage this intriguing history, well known Italian scientist Gerolamo Cardano appeared on the scene.

After unsuccessful attempts to find a method of solving cubic equations, Cardano in 1539 tried to reach Tartaglia, who was famous due to winning a contest on solving cubics, and tried to get him to divulge the method. By Cardano's request his friend met with Tartaglia in Venice an asked on behalf of "an honest name of the physician from Milan, Gerolamo Cardano" to give him the rule of cubic equation solution for publication in a book. Tartaglia responded negatively: "Let know his serenity that if I would like to publish the result, I will publish it in my own book, not in somebody's book!"

Nevertheless, Tartaglia eventually agreed after awhile getting Cardan to swear an oath that he would not publish the method until

Tartaglia had himself published it. Tartaglia agreed to open his secrets to Cardano after the last swear an oath of the following contents:

I swear to you, by God's holy Gospels, and as a true man of honor, not only never to publish your discoveries, if you teach me them, but I also promise you, and I pledge my faith as a true Christian, to note them down in code, so that after my death no one will be able to understand them.

Gerolamo Cardano
(1501-1576)

Cardano was one of the most educated scientists of his time. He was simultaneously mathematician and mechanist, physician and alchemist, chiropractic and personal astrologist of the Pope of Rome. By the way, once he compiled the Jesus Christ horoscope for what Saint Inquisition arrested him and kept some time in its.

Great German philosopher and mathematician Gottfried Wilhelm Leibniz told about him: "Cardano was a great man even with all his deficiencies; wihtout them he would be fineness".

For more details, see Chapter "Pantheon".

There was a brief correspondence between Cardano and Tartaglia because Cardano found a number of examples where Tartaglia idea did not work. In particular, in 1539 Cardano wrote:

Dismissing mental tortures, and multiplying $5+\sqrt{-15}$ *by* $5-\sqrt{-15}$, *we obtain* $25-(-15)$. *Therefore the product is* 40. .... *and thus far does arithmetical subtlety go, of which this, the extreme, is, as I have said, so subtle that it is useless.*

Notice that it was written when imaginary numbers still were not known to mathematicians!

In the same letter to Tartaglia Cardano wrote:

I have sent to enquire after the solution to various problems for which you have given me no answer, one of which concerns the cube equal to an unknown plus a

> *number. I have certainly grasped this rule, but when the cube of one-third of the coefficient of the unknown is greater in value than the square of one-half of the number, then, it appears, I cannot make it fit into the equation.*

One can see that it is a verbal formulation of existence of the conditions of solutions in real numbers.

Tartaglia by this time greatly regretted telling Cardano the method and responded him in rather venomous words:

> *... and thus I say in reply that you have not mastered the true way of solving problems of this kind, and indeed I would say that your methods are totally false.*

Anyway, in 1545 Cardano published his book "*Ars Magna*" ("*Great Art*"), in which he described the method of solving of cubic equation (the so-called "Cardano's Formula"). In the same book, there was the discovery done by Cardano's pupil Luigio Ferrari[19], who had found the method of solving equations of the fourth power.

It is necessary to notice that Cardano in the preface of his book made an acknowledgement to Tartaglia and Ferrari. About Tartaglia he wrote:

> *... not I but my friend Tartaglia should be honored for discovery such a beautiful and wonderful method. This discovery is a real God's gift and the proof of Tartaglia's perfect power of wisdom.*

Nevertheless, after the book publication Tartaglia accused Cardano in breaking the oath, and long and severe fight between two scientists had begun. Tartaglia declared that Cardano had robbed him. Luigi Ferrari, trying to protect his mentor, challenged Tartaglia to a public dispute on "geometry, arithmetic and related disciplines like astrology, music and so on".

Moreover, Ferrari wrote in 1547:

> *Four years ago when Cardano was going to Florence and I accompanied him, we saw at Bologna Hannibal Della Nave, a clever and humane man who*

[19] **Luigi (Lodovico) Ferrari** (1522-1565) was an Italian scholar who started as Cardano's secretary and went on to devise the solution of the quartic equation.

showed us a little book in the hand of Scipione del Ferro, his father-in-law, written a long time ago, in which that discovery was elegantly and learnedly presented.

This dispute took place in Milan in 1548. Tartaglia had lost that and this spoiled his academic status. After this he began to translate Archimedes and Euclid and had written his fundamental work "General Tractate on Numbers and Measure" (*Generale trattato de numeri e misure*) dealt with various problems of arithmetic, algebra and geometry.

The name "Cardano Formula" has been firmly consolidated for the formula for solution of the cubic equation. However, who knows: maybe if there would be no that long battle between Tartaglia and his opponent, after the Cardano's preface to his book, where all honor of the solution has been given to Tartaglia, the formula would bear his name and we would call it "Tartaglia's Formula"? Who knows…

Complexity of the rules describing the solution of cubic equations led to the necessity of notation improvement. The process has been during almost a century. At last, in the end of XVI century French mathematician François Viette introduced literal notations.

François Viette (or Vieta)
(1540-1603)

French mathematician made a significant input in algebra development. He is also referred as "Father of Algebra" due to his introducing of modern algebraic notations.

A jurist by education, he all his free time devoted to mathematics and astronomy.

He was called by his contemporaries "Apollonius Gallus" after great Greek geometer, astronomer, and mathematician Apollonius of Perga. (Gallia was the ancient name of the territory of France.)

In devising technical terms derived from the Greek he seems to have aimed at making them as unintelligible as possible. He proposed to denote unknown quantities by the capital vowels A, E, I, O, etc., and unknown quantities by the capital consonants B, C, D, etc.

He also introduced brief notations for arithmetical operations.(Before authors used their own notations, i.e. there were no "standardization".)

In the middle of XVII century due to French scientist Rene Descartes, algebraic symbolic possessed the form that was very close to that used by us now. Thus, algebra got universal "language of communication".

Rene Descartes

(1596 - 1650)

Outstanding French philosopher, mathematician, physicist and physiologist. Got his education at the Jesuit college. Fought during the 30-Year War. Since age 35 he lived in Holland, where he published his main works.

At age 55 he was invited to Sweden by the Queen. He caught a cold in Sweden and died.

He founded analytical geometry (with the Cartesian coordinates). The name of philosophical teaching – Cartesianism – originated from the Latin spelling of his name *Renatus Cartesius.* This philosophical school used Descartes famous motto:

"*Cogito ergo sum*" ("*I think therefore I am*").

Not in vain Nikolai Lobachevsky[20] told once: "Similarly as gift of words make us richer with others' opinions, the language of mathematical symbols is even more explicit and perfect for transferring concepts and new discoveries from one man to another".

Thus, arithmetic generated algebra. In the same manner, algebra generated abstract algebra!

[20] **Nikolai Ivanovich Lobachevsky** (1792 - 1856) was a great Russian mathematician, the creator of Lobachevsky's (non-Euclidian) geometry. He was outstanding philosopher.

A new mathematical branch has been appeared – the Group Theory. French scientist Evarist Galois was the first who connected the Group Theory with another branch of the abstract algebra – the Field Theory. That new theory is called now the Galois' Theory.

To penetrate more or less deep into this area is not acceptable thing for a popular book. However, it is absolutely impossible to leave aside one of the brightest figure of history of mathematics.

Evarist Galois
(1811-1832)

French mathematician whose works on the theory of algebraic equations laid a basis for development of modern algebra.

Evarist Galois had been killed at a duel when he was only 21 years old...

He left a few very short and compact works that were not understood at his time. His works had been published only in 1846.

For more details, see Chapter "Pantheon".

2. We were not taught this at school

2.1. Numbers, which are complex by definition

Evidently, the first numbers of very strange nature (that later were called "imaginary numbers") were discovered by Italian engineer and mathematician Gerolamo Cardano. In his book "Ars Magna" ("Great Work") published in 1545, he solved the following system of algebraic equations:

$$X + Y = 10$$
$$XY = 40\ ,$$

and got solutions $x = 5 + \sqrt{-15}$, $y = 5 - \sqrt{-15}$, which, as it seemed then, had no sense at all. Cardano called square roots from negative numbers as "sophistic numbers". He found them useless and tried to avoid them, saying that they cannot be used for measurement of physical objects…

Nevertheless, the Gin had been released from the bottle": in 1572 Rafael Bombelli[21] in his book "Algebra" gave arithmetic of imaginary numbers which he developed. The beginning of the theory of complex numbers started.

The name "imaginary numbers" was coined in 1637 by Rene Descartes, and in 1777 Leonard Euler suggested to use letter "*i*" (the first letter of the word "imaginary") for notation of "imaginary unit" ($\sqrt{-1}$).

Leonard Euler
(1707–1783)

One of the greatest mathematicians of the new history. He was born and educated in Switzerland then had been working in St. Petersburg Academy in Russia then moved for 25 years to Germany, and came back to Russia. During his last 17 years in Russia, being absolutely blind, he almost two-folded his scientific heritage: he dictated his works to his son and two assistants all day long.

He contributed a lot in various spheres of science and mathematics: in calculus combinatorics, probability theory, mechanics optics, astronomy, physics and even in theory of music.

For more details, see Chapter "Pantheon" in Book 2.

Third symbol found common usage due to Karl Gauss, who also introduced in 1831 a term "complex numbers".

Johann Carl Friedrich Gauss
(1777-1855)

Sometimes referred as the *princeps mathematicorum* (in Latin means "the foremost") and "greatest mathematician since antiquity".

For more details, see Chapter "Pantheon" in Book 5.

Then Leonard Euler expanded concepts of logarithm on complex numbers and in 1776 invented a new method of integrating with the use of complex variables.

Later Abraham de Moivre[22] in 1707 showed how to take roots of a natural power from complex numbers. He wrote a complex number in the trigonometric form as $z = r(\cos\varphi + i\sin\varphi)$ where r was some real number. He proved that for any natural number, it was possible to write $(r(\cos\varphi + i\sin\varphi))^n = r^n(\cos n\varphi + i\sin n\varphi)$.

In 1748 Euler gave a formula that connected two presentations of a complex number, both in trigonometric and exponential forms:

$$e^{i\varphi} = \cos\varphi + i\sin\varphi.$$

For the sake of justice, notice that factually this formula was first proven by Roger Kots[23] in 1714. He gave the formula in logarithmic form:

$$\ln(\cos(\varphi) + i\sin(\varphi)) = i\varphi.$$

With the help of Euler's formula the procedure of powering a complex number in an arbitrary power became understandable and formally clear:

$$\left(e^{i\varphi}\right)^n = e^{in\varphi}.$$

However, neither Euler, nor Cotes did not imagine a geometric interpretation of the obtained formula. Presentation complex numbers

[21] **Rafael Bombelli** (1526–1572) was an Italian mathematician and engineer.

[22] **Abraham de Moivre** (1667-1754) was a French mathematician famous for de Moivre's formula and for his work on the normal distribution and probability theory.

[23] **Roger Cotes** (1682-1716) was an English mathematician, known for working closely with Isaac Newton by proofreading the second edition of his famous book "Principia". He also invented the formulas known as Newton-Cotes formulas and first introduced what is known today as Euler's formula.

on the complex plane appeared only half a century later, in 1799 in the work by Caspar Wessel.[24], which was published in Dutch Royal Academy of Sciences.

Geometrical presentation of complex numbers is often called an "Argan's diagram" after Argan[25], who published in 1806 and 1814 two works, in which he independently got the same results as Wessel.

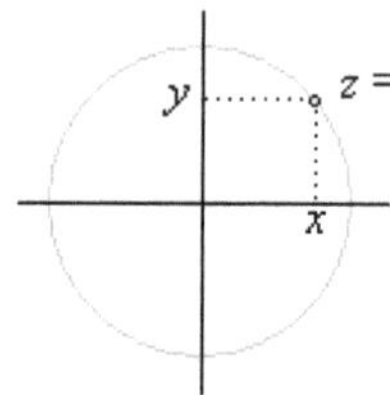

Argan's diag

Later it was found that even more convenient to depict a complex number by vector $\overline{0z}$ rather than by point *z*.

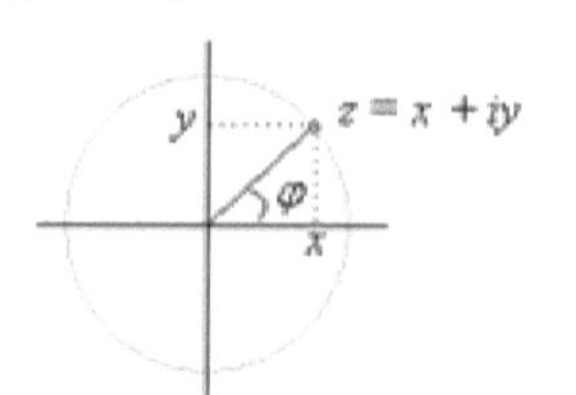

With such interpretation summation and extraction of complex numbers coincide with correspondent operations over vectors.

Vector $\overline{0z}$ can be defined not only by coordinates *x* and *y*, but also by its length *r* and angle □ which it forms with the positive direction of the abscissa.

The arithmetical theory of complex numbers had been developed by William Hamilton[26] in 1837 годy. He also developed a generalization of complex numbers by introducing "quaternion", which possesses quite strange for normal people property: their product is non-commutative, i.e. speaking in common language, the product depends on their order in the operation. However, to enter into the "algebraic jungle" would be almost impolite in respect to reader...

[24] **Caspar Wessel** (1745 - 1818) was a Norwegian-Danish mathematician and geodesist.
[25] **Jean Robert Argand** (1768–1822) was a Swiss amateur mathematician.
[26] **William Rowan Hamilton** (1805 -1865) was an Irish mathematician, physicist, and astronomer who made important contributions to the development of optics, dynamics, and algebra. He became Professor of Dublin University at age 22, at age 31 he became the President of the Irish Royal Academy of Sciences.

2.2. Tree Ancient problems

Three classical unsolvable problems of Ancient Greece mathematics influenced very much on the development of geometry:

- Circle quadrature,
- Three section of an angle
- Doubling a cube.

(Very often to these problems, the problem of construction of right septogram is added.)

Why and how unsolvable problems could help to development of geometry?

Let us recollect an old story about David Hilbert[27]. Once being asked: solution what a problem would be most useful for mathematics, immediately responded: "To catch a fly on the inverse site of the Moon!" Then he explained amazed audience: "The problem itself has no sense at all. However, imagine what kind of powerful and new methods should be invented to solve this problem. And in addition, how many other important discoveries we will be forced to make!"

Thus, you could imagine how much mathematics has got attempts to catch these "three geometrical flies" during thousands of years!

Circle quadrature

Problem of quadrature of the circle is the construction with a ruler and dividers such a square, which has an equal area with the given circle.

Methods of approximate construction of equal sized circle and square were known even Ancient Babylonians. The same is known about Ancient Egypt as we can see from Rhind's papyrus[28] (about 2 millenniums

[27] **David Hilbert** (1862 -1943) was a German mathematician, recognized as one of the most influential and universal mathematicians of the 19th and early 20th centuries. He invented or developed a broad range of fundamental ideas.

[28] **The Rhind Mathematical Papyrus** is named after Alexander Henry Rhind, a Scottish antiquarian, who purchased the papyrus in 1858 in Egypt. Now the papyrus is

B.C.!), though the circle area was determined approximately as $64 / 81d^2$, where *d* is the circle diameter. Less exact approximation was known in Ancient India.

First time the problem of circle quadrature as a mathematical one was formulated by Anaxagoras[29], when he spent his days in jail.

The circle quadrature problem was evidently so popular that even Aristophanes[30] in his comedy "Birds" put in the lips of one of his personages, who was an agronomist (i.e. a man close to mathematics), the following monologue:

Take a ruler, draw a line,
And immediately a circle becomes a square,
In the middle we arrange a market
And from this place streets will run –
Just like the Sun: it's round itself
Though its rays are straight!..

One of the first who began to construct equal size curve-lined figures and triangles was Hippocrates of Chios[31].

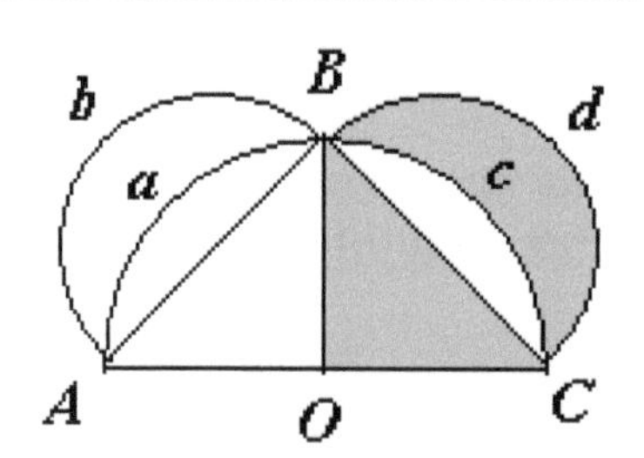

Let us follow one of his constructions. On segment *AO* construct half circle *AaBcC*. Then on sides *AB* and *BC* of isosceles triangle *ABC* construct two half circles: *AbB* and *BdC*, respectively. New curve-lined figures

---

now kept in the British Museum in London..

[29] **Anaxagoras of Clazomenae** (500 - 428 BC) was an ancient Greek mathematician, astronomer and pre-Socratic philosopher. Explaining such events as Sun and Moon eclipses, earthquakes, etc. by natural causes, he was convicted for unrespect of gods. He was condemned to death and only Pericle, who was the ruler in Athens, could protect the philosopher: the death verdict was replaced by proscription from Athens. "Not I who lost Athens, but Athenians lost me" – proudly claimed Anaxagoras.

[30] **Aristophanes** (456 - 386 BC) was an ancient Greek comic playwrit of ancient Athens. He is also known as the Father of Comedy. His first play he wrote at age 17.

[31] **Hippocrates of Chios** (470 - 400 BC) was an ancient Greek mathematician (geometer) and astronomer. The author of the first ever systematic work on geometry (unfortunately did not come to us). *Do not confuse with Hippocrates of Cos ("father of medicine"), who lived about a century earlier!*

AbBa и *BcCd* are called "Hippocrates' moons". It occurs that the shadowed area of the "moon" equals to the shadowed area of the corresponding triangle *OBC*.

By Pythagoras Theorem we have:

$$(AC)^2 = (AB)^2 + (BC)^2 = 2(BC)^2$$

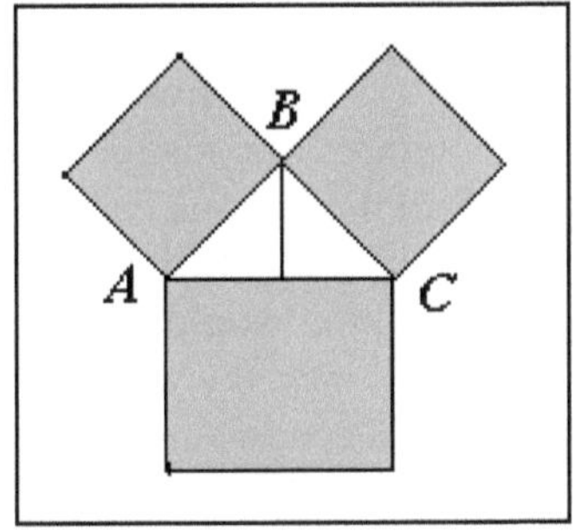

Hippocrates proved that the ratio of areas of two circles is equal to the ratio of areas of two squares which sides are equal to diameters of corresponding circles. So, the area of sector *OBcC* equals area of half a circle *BdC* with diameter *BC*. If from these equal six figures ozone extracts area *BcC*, then in result we obtain that area of triangle *BOC* equals to the area of "moon" *BcCd*.

In his attempts to solve circle quadrature problem, Hippocrates found many other interesting results. He did not reach unreachable solution but his name as one of the greatest geometer has come to us through millenniums.

At last, in 1667 James Gregory[32] gave a proof that the circle quadrature problem had no solution in his work "Vera Circuli et Hyperbolae Quadratura" ("The True Squaring of the Circle and of the Hyperbola"). Though his proof was not too strong, it was a very important step forward. (Then transcendent numbers which are non-algebraic, were unknown, therefore segments of such length cannot be "constructed" on the plane.)

Johann Lambert[33] in 1768 proved tha number π is tansidental though such numbers wereunknown at all atvthe time.

---

[32] **James Gregory** (1638 - 1675) was a Scottish mathematician and astronomer, creator of a mirror telescope.

[33] **Johann Heinrich Lambert** (1728 -1777) was a German mathematician, physicist, astronomer and philosopher. Being a son of a tailor, he was forced to quit a school at age 12 and was self-educated. Most important scientific input lies in photometria, "father" of which he is called. He proved that number "pi" is irrational. He introduced sinus and cosinus, anticipated many of John Bull ideas in the logic algebra. Member of Berlin

It was needed more than a century to make another step. In 1882 Ferdinand Lindemann[34] strongly proved that the circle quadrature problem is non-solvable and show that number "pi" is transcendent.

Thus it was shown that the problem cannot be solved with the use only a ruler and a divider.

> The circle quadrature problem generated not less maniacal attempts to construct a square with the area equal the area of a given circle than the famous Fermat Theorem.
>
> The formulation of the problem is so simple that one expects that a solution would be also simple…
>
> By the way, in spite of the strong solution of impossibility more than a century ago, attempts of solving this problem still continue...

Angle trisection

This problem's roots are also in Ancient World: How to divide an angle into three equal angles with the use only a ruler and a divider?

There are some special cases where such solution could be reached. For instance, to trisect a right angle (90^0) could do even Pythagoreans who knew that an inner angle of equilateral triangle equals 60^0. In this case it was enough to be able to find a bisectrissa in the triangle that can be done with the help of a ruler and a divider.

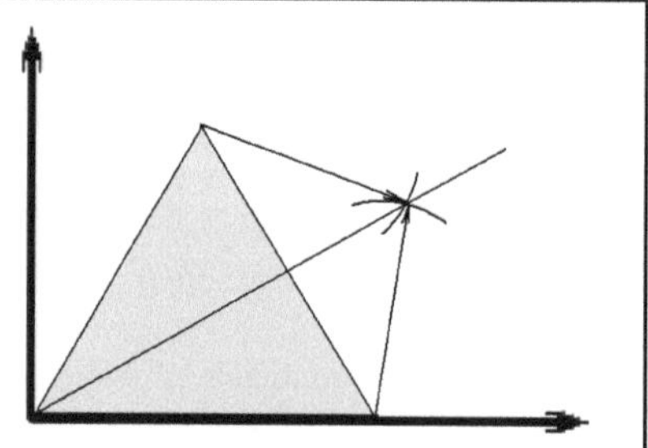

The trisection problem appears solvable for particular cases (for instance for angles of $\frac{\pi}{4n}$ where n is a natural number different from 3). However, the angle trisection problem cannot be solved only wit

Academy of Sciences..

[34]**Carl Louis Ferdinand von Lindemann** (1852-1939) was a German mathematician.

the help of a ruler and a divider that was the common tools of Ancient Greeks.

Archimedes' solution

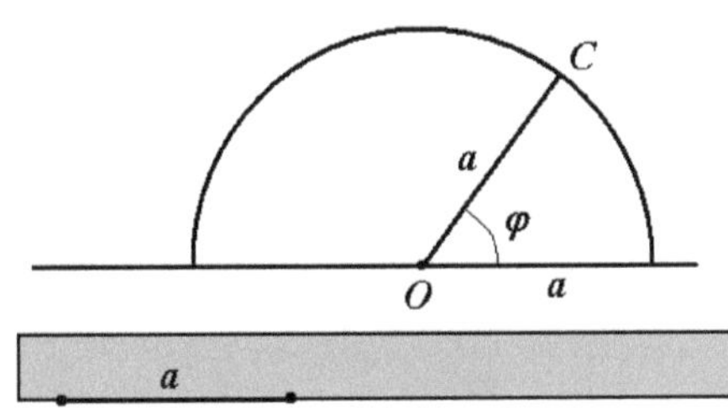

The problem of an angle trisection in contrast to the problem of circle quadrature was not just an exercise for an inquisitive mind: architects and constructors should solve this problem in their everyday job.

However, what to do is an angle is arbitrary? What to do? And you have only a ruler and a divider…

As Russian say, "if it is impossible but you desire it too much, then it is possible". However, in this case a wise brain of Archimedes head is needed in addition!

Probably, pure engineering problems pushed Archimedes to invent a convenient method of trisection of any angles though he used two minor ruses: he used a ruler with marks and a divider with a possibility to fix its "lega".

We should note that Archimedes, being a first class mathematician of all times, did not neglect for solution of practical problems to apply his head always fill with common sense and fantastic imagination.

Let us fix some distance a between a divider's legs. Led do two marks on a ruler on the same distance a.

Assume we need to trisect an arbitrary angle φ, formed by abscissa and a straight line coming from some arbitrary point O on axes x. Now let us make a half circle of fixed radius a with the center in O.

From point C where a side of a triangle crosses the circle, let us construct a straight line by the following manner. Let the ruler touches point C.

Then rotating and moving the ruler in such a way that its touching with point *C* preserves and at the same time, one of the mark will be on the circle and another on simultaneously will be on the axes *x*. The point where the ruler crosses the abscissa denotes by *A*, and cross of the ruler with the circle denote by *B*.

In result we come to the final graph presented below.

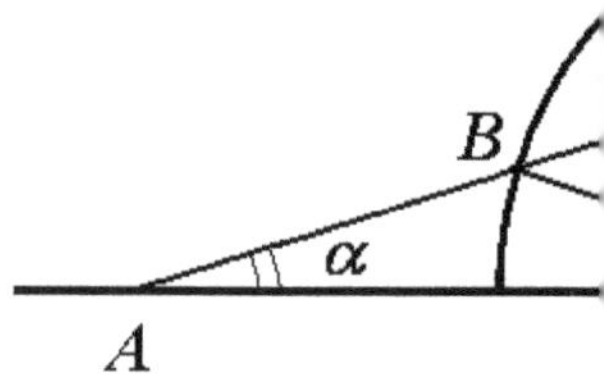

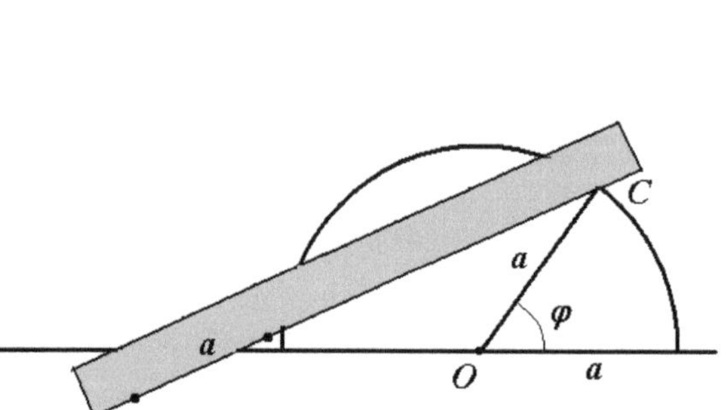

By construction, triangles *ABO* and *BOC* are isosceles and its sides are equal to the radius *a*. Angle *ABO* equals $\pi - 2\alpha$, so angle *OBC* equals $2\pi - (2\pi - 2\alpha) = 2\alpha$. Then for triangle *BOC* one can write: $\beta = 2\pi - 4\alpha$. At the same time, $\alpha + \beta + \varphi = 2\pi$, from where immediately follows:

$= 2\pi - (\alpha + \beta)$ $= 2\pi - (\alpha + 2\pi - 4\alpha) = 3\alpha$.

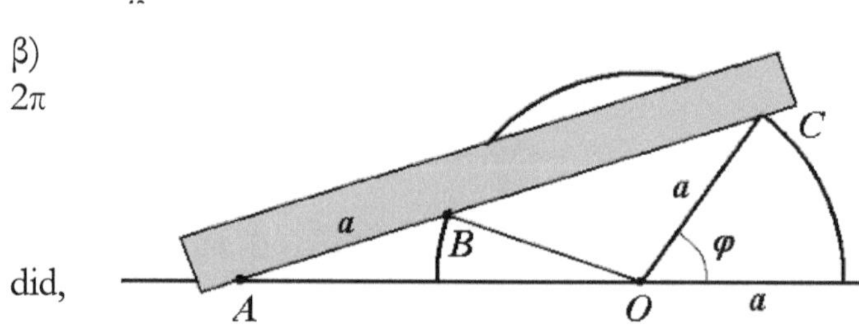

As everything Archimedes did, this is geniusly simple! He used only a ruler and a divider, though there was a minor ruse: the ruler was with two marks…

More about trisect rises

One of the most intriguing theorems in triangle geometry that is often called geometry pearl", is Morley's[35] Theorem. This theorem states the following:

> *In any triangle, the three points of intersection of the adjacent angle trisectors form an equilateral triangle.*

This triangle is called the Morley triangle.

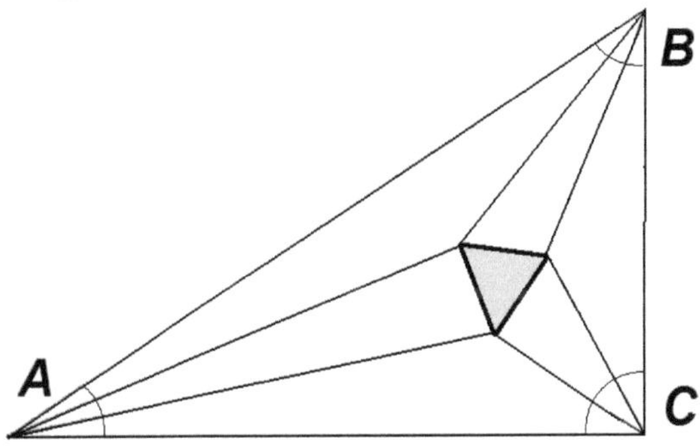

About this theorem Morley mentioned in 1804 to his friends just incidentally and published this result in 20 years and nobody knows why in Japan. It is to mention that Morley was an extraordinary person. For instance, he perfectly played chess and once even win a party with his colleague-mathematician Emanuel Lasker[36] who was a chess World champion during 27 years!

The contents of Morley's Theorem are illustrated by a simple graph that doesn't need any explanations.

---

[35] **Frank Morley** (1860 -1937) was an English-American mathematician, known mostly for his research in algebra and geometry.

[36] **Emanuel Lasker** (1868 -1941) was a German chess World Chess Champion and grandmaster, mathematician, and philosopher. He possessed the World chess championship since 1894 up to 1921 (longest possession of the World championship ever). With Hitler coming to the power in Germany, Lasker immigrated to the USA.

Thus for an arbitrary initial triangle, the inner triangle (gray in the figure) is always equilateral!

Frankly speaking, we don't wish to offend bisectrisses: they always possess a beautiful property that we know from our middle school. If one constructs perpendiculars to the sides from the point of bisectrisses crossing, then one gets a three ray star with equal length of rays. Actually we were told an equivalent statement: it is possible to draw a circle with the center coinciding with the point of bisectrisses intersection that touches all three sides simultaneously. Of course, lines connecting the center of the circle with sides are the shorter distances to the sides, so they are perpendiculars with the length equal radius.

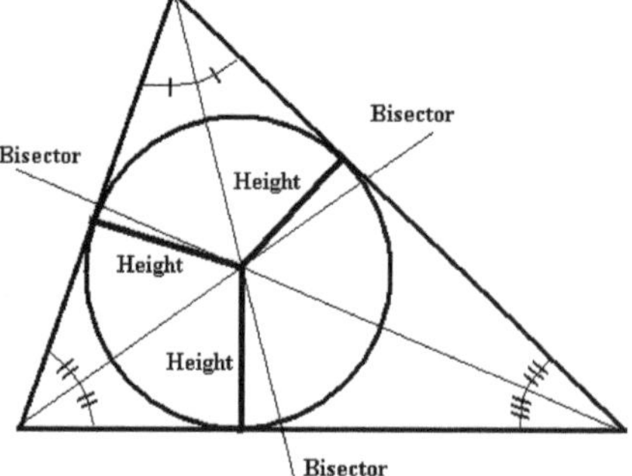

Doubling a cube

The problem of doubling cube volume with the help of a ruler and a divider is called "a problem of doubling a cube".

Let us begin from a distance… In ancient time constructions of various geometrical figures was in a sense a pursuit for selected people. Over the gate at Plato's Academy[37] there was an inscription: "*LET NONE IGNORANT OF GEOMETRY ENTER HERE*".

From time immemorial, the problem of doubling that square area had been solved with elegancy: one drew an "envelope" and one of its triangles attached to a square side, then such procedure continues. In result, one has two squares: a larger one consists of eight triangles and the smaller one does of the four ones.

---

[37] **Plato's Academy** was religious-philosophical school established by Ancient philosopher Plato in 385 BC near Athens in the grove where by legend mythological hero Academos had been buried. The name of the grove were put in the name of the school.

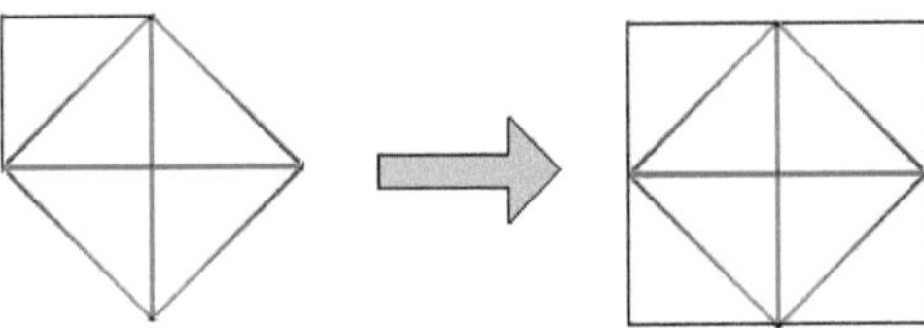

Let now come to a "minor" complication of the problem: we are interested in doubling a cube volume...

It is time to mention that in modern times the problem of circle quadrature was very popular though in Ancient times people paid more attention to the problem of doubling a cube volume.

By one of legends, well known mythological Crete's king Minos[38] ordered to build a tomb for his died son in Knoss, the capital of hid kingdom. The tomb had a form of a cube. When it had been constructed, Ninos ordered to double its volume.

Of course, this version is weak even by sense: why exactly as much as twice? If Minos so loved his don, it would be more reasonable to order to increase the tomb volume not less than twice. However, a myth is a myth, and we cannot give advices to the son of Seus...

By another version, that even is called Delosian since by legend citizens of Attica (Greek region containing Athens), trying to avoid a plague pandemic in V century B.C., asked the oracle of the island of Delos[39]. The oracle told them that Athenians incensed god Apollo and to calm him they should increase the Apollo temple twice as much though keeping the cubic form.

Athenians tried to solve the problem with pure geometrical methods with no success. (It was natural, since the problem cannot be solved with a ruler and a divider.) During the time of trying to solve the problem, they lost about the fourth of their entire population. Then they ask for help Plato. The great philosopher mentioned that gods punished Athenians, first of all, for their neglecting mathematics and lack of respect

[38] That same **Minos**, son of Zeus and Europe, whose wife Pasiphae, having "love affair" with the Crete's Bull, gave a birth to Minotaur, a monster with human body and bull's head (that monster lived in Labirint).

[39] **Delos** is a tiny Greek island, which by mythology is the birthplace of Apollo and Artemis. Now it is almost inhabitant.

to geometry. He solved the problem in practical way with the use a special tool with moving rulers.

Eudoxus'[40] pupil by the name of Menehem[41] gave the solution but not with using parable and hyperbole.

The first strong proof that this problem is unsolvable with pure geometric constructions was done only two millenniums later: it made Rene Descartes in 1637.

2.3. Pascal Triangles and its "relatives"

> Pascal Triangle is much more enigmatic than Bermuda Triangle!
>
> ***Unknown author***

In algebra and combinatorial analysis binomial coefficients play a special role. Probably most of you met them dealing with a *Newton binomial*: $(x+1)^n$, where n is an integer. These types of polynomials are presented below.

Newton Binomial	**Power**	**Binomial coefficients**
$(x+1)^0=1$	0	1
$x+1$	1	1<>1
$(x+1)^2=x^2+2x+1$	2	1<>2<>1
$(x+1)^3 =x^3+3x^2+3x+1$	3	1<>3<>3<>1
$(x+1)^4=x^4+4x^3+6x^2+6x\ 1$	4	1<>4<>6<>4<>1
$(x+1)^5=x^5+5x^4+10x^2+5x+1$	5	1<>5<>10<>5<>1
$(x+1)^6=x^6+6x^5+15x^4+20x^3$ $+15x^2+6x+1$	6	1<>6<>15<>20<>15<>6<>1
…	…	…

[40] **Eudoxus of Cnidus** (408 – 355 BC) was an ancient Greek astronomer, mathematician, physician, scholar and student of Plato.

[41] **Menehem** (IV BC) was an ancient Greek mathematician, a follower of the Plato's school.

In general form, the Newton binomial can be written in the following form:

$$(a+b)^n = C_n^0 a^n b^0 + C_n^1 a^{n-1} b^1 + C_n^2 a^{n-2} b^2 + ... + C_n^{n-1} a^{n-(n-1)} b^{n-1} + C_n^n a^{n-n} b^n$$

where C_n^k is *k*-th by order from the beginning binomial coefficient of the open form of the binomial of the *n*-th power.

Notice that a binomial coefficient C_n^k is denoted as $\binom{n}{k}$.

Thus, it is possible to write using the summation symbol:

$$(a+b)^n = \sum_{k=0}^{n} C_n^k a^{n-k} b^k .$$

Thus, where from did binomial coefficients appear?

In European mathematics the method of calculation of binomial coefficients became popular after Blaise Pascal's book "Treatise on the Arithmetical Triangle" (*Traité du triangle arithmétique*). He suggested a simple and visual algorithm of binomial coefficient calculation that later was called "Pascal's Triangle".

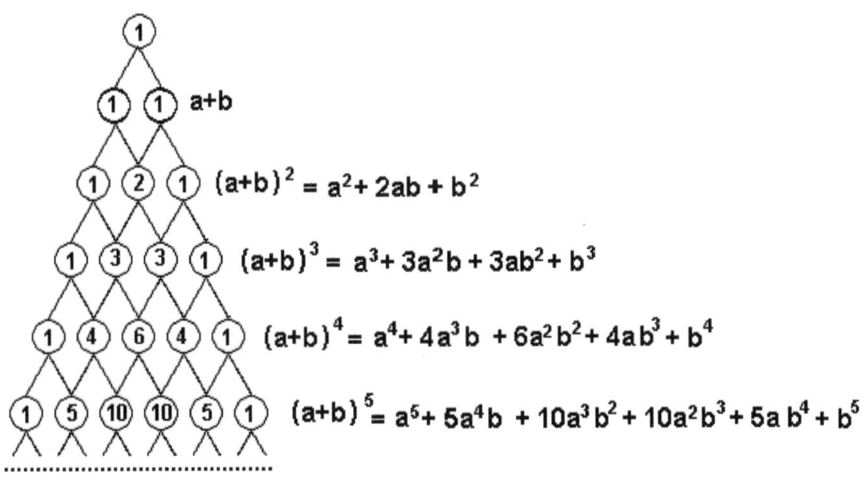

The algorithm of Pascal's Triangle construction is clear from the figure: a number in any circle can be obtained as the sum of quantities in the two immediately foregoing circles. In other words, each element of the triangle is defined by the rule:

$$L_{n+1,k}=L_{n,k-1}+L_{n,k} ,$$

where *n* is a number of row and *k* is the ordering unit number from the left of the row beginning.

Blaise Pascal

(1623-1662)

One of the best mathematicians of his time.

When he was only 12 years old, without any help, he had perfectly studied geometry. Being 16 years old he published his work on geometry that astonished Rene Descartes who was one of the greatest mathematicians in whole mathematical history.

For more details, see Chapter "Pantheon".

For justice purposes, we should notice that analogous (probably, even almost identical) method of binomial coefficients calculation was discovered in Europe 100 years before Pascal was born: it was published in 1533 in "Cosmography" by Peter Apian[42]. Thus, these important mathematical results should be re-discovered later…

It is interesting to notice a not so well known fact: in China at the end of the Sung dynasty ruling (960–1279), Chinese already had a kind of "Siam twin" of the Pascal's Triangle.

Three names of Chinese mathematicians have to be mentioned in this connection. The first is Chia Hsien (circa 1100 A.D.) who wrote a book called "Shih-so suan-shu" in which he described the tabulation system for

[42] **Peter** (**Bennewitz**) **Apian**, or (in Latin) **Petrus Apianus** (1495-1552) was a German geographer and cartographer.

unlocking binomial coefficients. Yang Hui basing on the Chia Hsien's work listed the binomial coefficients up to $(a+b)^6$ in 1261. About forty years later, in 1303, Chu Shih-chieh in his book "*Precious Mirror of the Four Elements*" developed the method up to $(a+b)^8$.

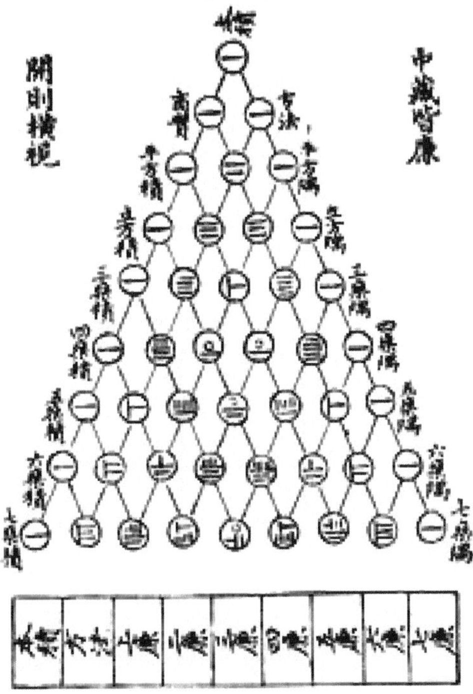

Figure from the Chu Shih-chieh's book

In Chinese mathematical literature to this day, they call the array of numbers Yanghui's Triangle.

Thus, the triangle of binomial coefficients was discovered in Europe almost half a millennium years later that its first appearance in China!

The Pascal Triangle can be presented in a different way, putting the triangle on its side. Such a presentation might be useful for further considerations.

1	1	1	1	1	1	1	1	...
	1	2	3	4	5	6	7	...

		1	3	6	10	15	21	...
			1	4	10	20	35	...
				1	5	15	35	...
					1	6	21	...
						1	7	...
							1	...
1	2	4	8	16	32	64	128	...

It is easy to note that rows in this table correspond to horizontal layers in a common Pascal Triangle. The binomial coefficients are calculated on the basis of such table as follows:

(a) for inner cells z

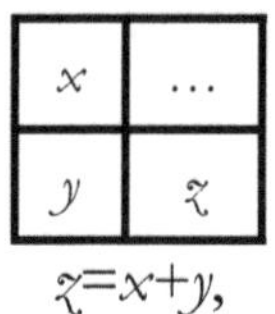

$z=x+y$,

(b) for "border" cells values are always equal to 1.

In other words, each element of the table is calculated with the use of the Pascal's rule: $L_{n+1,k}=L_{n,k-1}+L_{n,k}$ with initial conditions $L_{1,0}=1$, $L_{1,1}=2$ and $L_{0,k}=0$.

The binomial coefficients can be read by columns: for $(x+1)^0$, the first column consists of a single element ("1"); for $(x+1)^1$, the second column consists of two elements ("1, 1"); for $(x+1)^2$, the third column consists of three elements ('1, 2, 1'), and so on.

If one summates the binomial coefficient column after column, we get a set of numbers that present powers of 2: $2^0=1$, $2^1=2$, $2^2=4$, $2^3=8$, $2^4=16$, $2^5=32$, $2^6=64$, ... and so on. Of course, it becomes obvious if one take $x=1$ for the Newton binomial $(x+1)^n$ because in that case $(1+1)^n = 2^n$.

Let us move one cell to the right at each row relatively the previous (upper) row. As the result we got after summation of columns Fibonacci numbers

1	1	1	1	1	1	1	1	1	1	1	...
		1	2	3	4	5	6	7	8	9	...
				1	3	6	10	15	21	28	...
						1	4	10	20	35	...
								1	5	15	...
										1	...
1	1	2	3	5	8	13	21	34	55	89	...

Such a presentation of the Pascal's Triangle permits to construct many interesting new sequences of numbers. For instance, with this table one can easily to construct a generalized Fibonacci sequence when a rabbit becomes mature only at k-th month.

2.4. The Great, or Last Fermat's Theorem

In connection with the Pythagoras Theorem, an interesting question arises: how many numbers satisfy equation

$$x^2 + y^2 = z^2 ?$$

(Here x and y might be interpreted as length of cathetus, and z as a hypotenuse of direct triangles.) This question irritated many Ancient and Medieval scientists.

A set of such integer numbers $(x, \; y, \; z)$ is called a Pythagorean Triplet.

Euclid proved that there are infinitely many such Pythagorean Triplets. The concept of his proof is not so simple, so we omit it. Let us write down the solution: for any Pythagorean Triplet the following conditions are necessary

$$x=l(m^2 - n^2), \quad y=2lmn, \quad z=l(m^2 + n^2),$$

where l, m, n are natural numbers and in addition $m>n$.

For instance, let us illustrate the result of the Euclidian proof on a "classical" Pythagorean Triplet (3, 4, 5). This triplet is obtained if one choose l=1, m=2, and n=1. If one chose l=1, m=3, and n=1, then the Pythagorean Triplet is (6, 8, 10), i.e. a new triangle is similar to the first one though each its side is twice as much as in the first case. For l=1, m=3, and n=2, the obtained triangle has sides 5, 12, and 13.

The story with Pythagorean Triplets did not vanish without trace.

Problem with Pythagorean Triplets is relatively simple. However, if one tries to increase power from 2 to 3, and… the problem becomes extremely complex!

In 1636, i.e. almost two millenniums after Pythagoras, French mathematician Pierre Fermat formulated a statement that later was called the Great, or Last Fermat Theorem. He claimed that equation $x^n+y^n=z^n$ has no solution if $n > 2$. The poof of this statement appeared unimaginably difficult.

Pierre de Fermat

(1601-1665)

French mathematician who was simultaneously an adviser to the Parliament of the city of Toulouse. Fermat made a significant input into analytical geometry, theory of numbers, and calculus. His name associates with the most intriguing theorem in entire history of mathematics.

His discoveries in the numbers theory influenced on the development of this branch of knowledge for centuries.

For more details, see Chapter "Pantheon".

One of the most fruitful and erudite mathematicians of the 18th century, Leonard Euler proved this theorem for powers equal 3 and 4, however, his method did not work for higher powers…Then Antoine Legendre[43] proved the theorem for the power of 5, and Gustav Direchlet[44] did it for the power of 7… However, it is impossible to prove infinite number of particular cases! The proof should be for a general case.

Let us try to illustrate this problem in graphical way. Start with Pythagorean Triplets: one needs to find two squares, consisting of unitary squares (1x1), that a larger square could be built from all unitary squares of the first two ones. For instance, take squares 6x6 and 8x8.

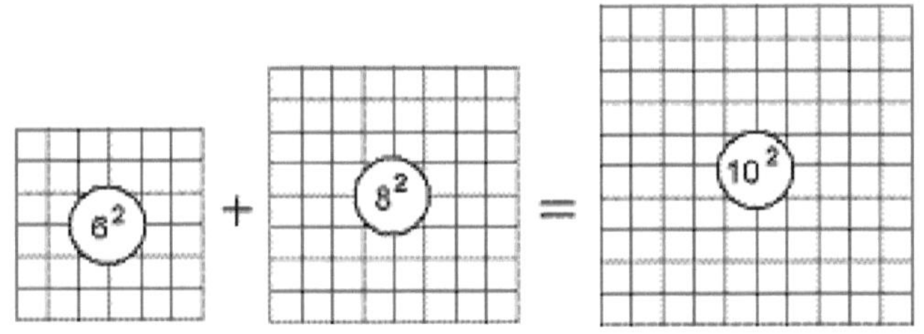

Now let us try to consider an analogous situation when $n = 3$. In this case, one needs to build a larger cube from unitary cubes (1x1x1) that constitute two smaller cubes. It occurs that all attempts finish with mischance: one has some extra unitary cubes or there is a lack of several unitary cubes. Sometimes, one is "very close" to the solution. For instance, let us take two cubes 6x6x6 and 8x8x8. Finally we construct "almost" a cube 9x9x9: there is a deficit in one extra unitary cube 1x1x1! (Of course, one is lucky if could find even such "approximate solution"!)

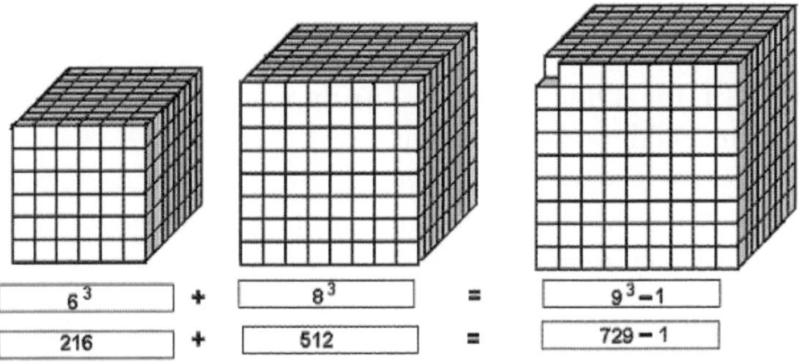

[43] **Adrien-Marie Legandre** (1752-1833) was an an outstanding French mathematician.
[44] **Peter Gustav Direchlet** (1805-1859) was an outstanding German mathematician.

In accordance with the Great Fermat Theorem there is no such three integer numbers that satisfy equation $x^3 + y^3 = z^3$.
This statement is justice for any integer power n larger than 2.

The Great Fermat Theorem is, probably, the most known mathematical theorem that is familiar even for people not too close to mathematics. Simplicity of formulation of the theorem deceived a number of people who thought that it should lead to a simple solution.

As soon the formulation of the Fermat Theorem became known, thousands of professional and amateur mathematicians spent years and years in fruitless attempts to find the proof of it. Some have lost their mind no literally but actually: hospitals for mental disease became to have a new category of sick people – "Fermatists", who tried to find the proof of Fermat Theorem with maniacal persistency…

Mathematical departments all European universities were overwhelmed with myriads of proofs, thousands of mathematicians spent their time for expertise…

It is said that in some universities, especially overloaded with "Fermatists' works", there were special in advance prepared letters of response:

Dear ___________!
In your proof of the Fermat Theorem on __page on __ line from above I formula:____ there has been found the following error: ______.

It is time to notice that Pierre Fermat poured oil on the flame: on the margin of the Diophantus's[45] "Arithmetica" that was his beloved book from the childhood, he wrote in Latin:

"*It is impossible to separate a cube into two cubes, or a fourth power into two fourth powers, or in general, any power higher than the second into two like powers. I have discovered a truly marvelous proof of this, which this margin is too narrow to contain*".

---

[45] **Diophantus of Alexandria** (325-409) was a famous Ancient mathematician who wrote a manuscript that contain entire mathematical knowledge of the time. Introduced the so-called Diophantine equations. He was the first who use literal notations in algebra.

Generation after generation, mathematicians tried to prove the Fermat Theorem or to find s controversial example.

Once famous mathematician David Hilbert was asked why he never tried to prove the Fermat's Theorem. He answered: "Before beginning I should put in three years of intensive study, and I haven't that much time to squander on a probable failure".

After years of collective attempts to proof the Fermat's Theorem, many people decided that the proof is impossible. Simultaneously some sick "Fermatists" told even that it is not less than "Devil's machinates"...

In the beginning of the last century, a rich industrial magnate and professor of mathematics Paul Wolfskehl[46] was one of those who tried to find the proof of the Great Fermat's Theorem. As a researcher he did nothing, however his name will be associated with that theorem for a long time because he generated a new wave of attempts to solve the problem.

This near-mathematical problem began in a very romantic way: Wolfskehl had unlucky love and was rejected by the subject of his heart... He was in desperate situation and even decided to make a suicide. He began with typical accuracy and pedantry of a German (and in addition – mathematician!) his preparations to suicide. He decided to shot himself in a temple when the clock would chime midnight. As any normal suicide, he decided, first of all, to arrange all deeds: to compile a will, to write goodbye letters to friends and relatives. He had finished everything long time before midnight, so to shorten the time, he went to his study and became to look through mathematical journals. Accidentally he met a paper explaining why Augustine Cauchy[47] came to grief with his search of the Fermat's Theorem proof. He became interested in the paper, went to the desk and began to write down his own analysis of Cauchy's mistakes.

[46] **Paul Friedrich Wolfskehl** (1856-1906) was a German professor of mathematics who inherited a family bank after his father death. He bequeathed 100,000 marks (equivalent to almost $2,000,000 in today's money) to the first person to prove or disprove Fermat's Last Theorem.

[47] **Augustine Louis Cauchy** (1789-1857) was a French mathematician who introduced concept of continuality of functions and a limit at a point, gave integral definition as a limit of the sum, etc. He is also known of for his works in optics and elasticity.

He had finished his work … at the sunrise! He found that the time for suicide passed away, however he was not really sad of it. In such a way, mathematics saved the life of a man! He teared out his goodbye letters and destroyed the will.

As he found later, his arguments in that night paper were wrong, however, what did it mean in comparison with saved life!

Many years later, when Wolfskehl died, entire his family were in a shock: they\y found that a huge bulk of money – 100 thousand marks (huge money at the time!) were bequeathed to that who would have proved the Great Fermat's Theorem. That money was put on the account of Royal scientific society in Gettingen, and in the same time the Wolfskehl competition was announced. …

* * *

Anekdote: It is said that in 1980-s on the wall of New York underground the following inscription appeared: "Equation $x^n + y^n = z^n$ has no solutions in integers. I have discovered a truly marvelous proof of this, though I have no time to write this solution because my train is coming…"

So, people began to believe that there is no way to prove the enigmatic theorem… Nevertheless, it has been proven!

June 27, 1997 the Wolfskehl's prize has been presented to Andrew John Wiles, British mathematician who is working now at Princeton University.

Wiles was born in 1953 in Cambridge (England). He graduated from Cambridge University and was left there as scientific researcher. He heard about the Great Fermat's Theorem at age 10. After graduation he spent many years trying to solve the world-known problem, though keeping this fact in secret because he did not to earn a fame of one of thousand crazy "Fermatists".

When he became 35, wiles completely submerged in the solution of unsolvable problem. And in 7 years he presented to world mathematical community his results.

In 1994, Wiles made a presentation at Isaac Newton Institute at Cambridge. In a sense, a good time of presentation has been chosen: Paul Wolfskehl in his will announced the deadline of the competition– September 13, 2007.

The Wiles' presentation impressed everybody, and immediately a wire has been sent to the Wolfskehl Commission: the Great Fermat's Theorem has been proven at last! By the rules, the proof should be published and outstanding mathematicians should confirm correctness of the proof. In Wolfskehl's will for this procedure was given 2 years.

Wiles has published his solution in the same year. It was 200 pages proof! Mathematicians all around the World were excited, newspapers of all countries announced about such a historical event.

But... Very soon Wiles' colleagues have found fundamental mistake in his arguments, and the author has nothing more than to recall his work. He began checking and rechecking his proof. It takes about a year. A new version of the proof was again presented to the Mathematical community.

This time everything was absolutely correct!

PANTHEON

Omar Khayyam
(1048 - 1131)

Persian mathematician, astronomer and philosopher who made very much for algebra development.

For wide audience he is best known for his stanzas (quatrains) that were written in Farsi and now translated into all languages of the World.

All work of Khayyam – scientist and poet – is a wonderful phenomenon in history of culture of the people of Central Asia and entire Manhood.

Omar Khayyam was born in Nishapur to a prosperous tent maker (literally, "*al-khayyami*" means "*tent maker*"). His full name is Ghiyas al-Din Abu al-Fath Omar ibn Ibrahim Khayyam Nishaburi.

Exact date of his birth – May18, 1048 – was calculated by astronomers by saved horoscope which has been compiled by Omar himself.

Nishapur at the time was a capital of the Seljuk Empires, which expanded from Aegean Sea to Central Asia and the Caucasus. The city by its cultural and trade importance was a rival to Cairo or Baghdad.

Omar began his study at Nishapur madrasah and afterwards was sent by his parents to town of Balkh (present northern Afghanistan) and Samarkand (present Uzbekistan), studying under the perfect scholars.

At age of 17 he had reached deep knowledge in various areas: in algebra and in geometry, in physics and astronomy. He knew works of Ancient scientists – Archimedes, Euclid, Aristotle by Arabic translations. He was knowledgeable in medicine and astrology, knew theory of music. (There are some references of Khayyam Contemporaries that he wrote an original work on mathematical theory of music.)

He studied philosophy, theosophy, the Koran and history. Besides, he proficiently knew Arabic, had read a lot of Arabic literature, and had an ability to write verses.

Omar's contemporaries mentioned about his exclusive natural gifts.

Finishing his study, he wrote his first work on taking roots of power n from any integer positive N. This tractate "Difficulties of Arithmetic" has not been saved and we know about it only by references of his contemporaries. It is known that based on works of Indian mathematicians, Khayyam gave the method of solution of equations of the type $\tilde{o}^n = a$ with integer n. In the same work Omar gave the rule of writing the open form of binomial $(a+b)^n$ when n is integer (that we know as Newton's binomial).

Unfortunately, Omar Khayyam's works hundreds of years remained unknown to European mathematician dealing with algebra and non-Euclidian geometry. Thus, they were forced to repeat that long and hard way that had been already done by Khayyam about 5-6 centuries before.

During some disturbances in the Sultanate, Khayyam left the country and moved to Burkhart and Samarkand. At that time a scientist could devote himself to science only at the court of regional ruler. When Khayyam moved to Bukhara he found there a protege – Bukhara's Prince. Chroniclers of that time wrote that Omar was surrounded with honor and the Prince even let him sit down "on the throne with him".

About 1069 Khayyam wrote his famous work – "*Treatise on Demonstration of Problems of Algebra and Al-Muqabala*[48]" ("*Risalafi al-jabr wa al-muqabala*"). The date of writing the book was decided due to Omar's dedication of the book to Bukhara's Prince.

This work was his most substantial mathematical contribution and brought to its author honor and fame. Here he laid down the principles of algebra. It was the first attempt to give a classification of linear, quadratic and cubic equations (in total 25 types).In particular, he derived a geometrical method of cubic equations solving by intersecting a hyperbola with a circle. He also gave methods of solution equation of some higher orders.

In addition he discovered the binomial expansion. In the "*Treatise*", he also wrote on the triangular array of binomial coefficients known as Pascal's triangle. His method of quadratic equations solving is also similar to what is used today.

Omar Khayyam also had other notable work in geometry, specifically on the theory of proportions.

It is also known that Khayyam also wrote an original tractate on mathematical theory of music.

Like most mathematicians of the Medieval times, Omar Khayyam was also famous as an astronomer. In 1073, Sultan of the Seljuk Sultanate invited Khayyam to build an observatory in Isfahan. The scientist became a court mathematician and The Sultan put him close to himself.

By legend, the Sultan suggested Khayyam to be a ruler of his native Nishapur region. The scientist answered on this proposal: "I don't like to control people, to make orders and to forbid anything. I would like to dedicate entire my wisdom to serving the people!" The Sultan was astonished by such response and gifted Khayyam salary about 10000 golden dinars a year (huge money at the time!), so he could study and not to think about life problems.

Khayyam and his colleagues measured the length of the solar year as 365.24219858156 days (it is correct to six decimal places). This calendar

[48] *Al-Muqabala* means "balancing". It is a mathematical operation of transmitting an addendum from one side of an equation to another. For instance, equation $x^2 + 5 = 40x + 4x^2$ transforms to $5 = 40x + 3x^2$.

measurement has only a 1 hour error every 5,500 years, whereas the Gregorian Calendar, adopted in Europe five centuries later (!), has a 1 day error in every 3,330 years, though, naturally, the Khayyam's Calendar is harder to calculate. This calendar, known as Jalali calendar after the Sultan's name, had been accepted as the official Persian calendar.

In this calendar the lengths of the months can vary between 29 and 32 days depending on the moment when the sun crossed into a new zodiacal area. This calendar has been reformed only in 1925.

Omar Khayyam also built a star map (now lost), which was famous in the Persian and Islamic world. Unfortunately, this map has been lost and we have only written evidences about its existence.

He also estimated and proved that the universe is not moving around earth as was believed by all at that time. He constructed a revolving platform and simple arrangement of the star charts lit by candles around the circular walls of the room, he demonstrated that earth revolves on its axis, bringing into view on the sky different constellations throughout the night and day (i.e. during a one-day cycle). He also elaborated that stars are stationary objects in space.

18-year period of his life in Isfahan was the most effective and fruitful period of Khayyam's life.

In Medieval time, astronomy and astrology were like twins, moreover astrology was considered as one of "practical sciences". Due to his position at the Malik-Shah court, Omar became a court astrologer. His fame of and fortune-teller dispersed in the Sultanate. However, one of his friends wrote: "Though I was an eyewitness of predictions of the King of Wise (that was an honorable nickname of Omar Khayyam; before such title bore only Avicenna[49]), however I could not find a drop of believe in his own fortune-telling by stars".

In 1077 Khayyam had finished his brilliant mathematical work "*Commentaries on the difficult postulates of Euclid's book*" («*Sharh ma ashkala min musadarat kitab Uqlidis*»). One of the most important sections of the book is that with Khayyam's critics of famous Euclidean postulate about

[49] **Abu Ali al-Husayn ibn Abd Allah ibn Sina** known by his Latinized name **Avicenna (980-1037) was a** Persian astronomer, chemist, mathematician, physicist, theologian, poet, musician and foremost physician and philosopher of his time.

parallel lines. These ideas were far before the time, only later they entered Europe and influenced on the first steps of development of non-Euclidian geometry.

In 1080 Khayyam wrote a philosophical tractate in response of a letter of imam of one Persian province. The imam asked the scientist, whom he called "the King of philosophers of the West and East" to explain how Omar understood Allah's wisdom in the creation of the World and a man and what Omar thought about necessity of praying. That letter appeared not from nowhere: Omar Khayyam was well known by his blasphemous stanzas and direct anti-clerical statements.

The latter forced Khayyam openly declare his acceptance of main Islam religious postulates (what else could he do living in the country with a strong religious principles?

In his response Khayyam claimed himself as Avicenna's pupil and follower and dispose his viewpoints as Eastern Aristotelian ones. He confirmed that God is the Creator of everything but that existence of the World created by God controls by Nature's laws. His convictions, which were very often opposite to official Islam doctrine, Khayyam exposed brief and in moderate style and were written in Aesopian language.

However, the Sultan's protection saved the apostate from punishment. At the same time too many anti-religious Khayyam's verses were so popular among people that he was considered undesirable for Islam.

Unexpectedly, in 1092 under unclear circumstances the Sultan died and just a month before his vizier who was Khayyam's supporter, has been killed. The scientist position at the Sultan's court became wobbly.

Fearing open actions from Islam fanatics, Omar Khayyam undertook a long and difficult hajj (pilgrimage) to Mecca.

One of envy Islamic historians wrote: "When his contemporaries found his lack of believe that he tried to hide, he being afraid for his blood made a hajj. However, he did it not because his belief. … He has nobody comparable in astronomy and philosophy though he has no a gift to be obedient to God!"

When the throne again came into the hands of the former Sultan's son, he permitted Khayyam to come back to his native Nishapur. At this time he was about 70 years old.

Omar Khayyam made a number of discoveries in mathematics, astronomy, physics and other sciences. However, nobody should forget about his precious poetry heritage. His brilliant quatrains admire us by its beautiful lyrics, laconic manner and musical rhythm. Each his stanzas is an original micro-poem.

The Khayyam's poetry became known in Europe only in 1859, when Fitzgerald[50] published his 75 stanzas from "Rubayat[51]".

Though some consider Khayyam's poetry just a form of scientist leisure, it became one of treasures of the World literature.

This is the most impressive impression of Khayyam personality: the poet can think as a scientist, and the scientist can observe the World as a poet. The Khayyam's creativity is one of the most wonderful and enigmatic phenomenon in the history of Central Asia culture as well as entire Manhood.

Omar Khayyam's Rubaiyat

Some samples from Omar's poetry

[50] **Edward Marlborough Fitzgerald** (1809-1883) was an English writer, best known as the poet of the first and most famous English translation of Omar Khayyam's Rubaiat. This translation is considered as a chez d'ovre of British poetry of 19th century.

[51] **Rubai** (robaghi, robai) (plural in Arabic "rubaiyat") means "quadriple". It is a form of Eastern poetry (9th -12th centuries). It is a quadruplet with rhymes "a-a-b-a".

***

Dreaming when Dawn's Left Hand was in the Sky
I heard a Voice within the Tavern cry,
"Awake, my Little ones, and fill the Cup
Before Life's Liquor in its Cup be dry."

***

And those who husbanded the Golden Grain,
And those who flung it to the Winds like Rain,
Alike to no such aureate Earth are turn'd
As, buried once, Men want dug up again.

***

I sometimes think that never blows so red
The Rose as where some buried Caesar bled;
That every Hyacinth the Garden wears
Dropt in its Lap from some once lovely Head.

***

Ah! my Beloved, fill the Cup that clears
TO-DAY of past Regrets and future Fears-
To-morrow?--Why, To-morrow I may be
Myself with Yesterday's Sev'n Thousand Years.

***

Lo! some we loved, the loveliest and the best
That Time and Fate of all their Vintage prest,
Have drunk their Cup a Round or two before,
And one by one crept silently to Rest.

***

Oh, come with old Khayyam, and leave the Wise
To talk; one thing is certain, that Life flies;
One thing is certain, and the Rest is Lies;
The Flower that once has blown for ever dies.

***

There was a Door to which I found no Key:
There was a Veil past which I could not see:
Some little Talk awhile of ME and THEE
There seemed--and then no more of THEE and ME.

***

Ah, fill the Cup:--what boots it to repeat
How Time is slipping underneath our Feet:
  Unborn TO-MORROW and dead YESTERDAY,
Why fret about them if TO-DAY be sweet!

***

And if the Wine you drink, the Lip you press,
End in the Nothing all Things end in--Yes-
  Then fancy while Thou art, Thou art but what
Thou shalt be--Nothing--Thou shalt not be less.

***

Come, fill the Cup, and in the fire of Spring
Your Winter garment of Repentance fling:
  The Bird of Time has but a little way
To flutter--and the Bird is on the Wing.

***

A Book of Verses underneath the Bough,
A Jug of Wine, a Loaf of Bread--and Thou
  Beside me singing in the Wilderness--
Oh, Wilderness were Paradise enow!

***

Some for the Glories of This World; and some
Sigh for the Prophet's Paradise to come;
  Ah, take the Cash, and let the Credit go,
Nor heed the rumble of a distant Drum!

***

And those who husbanded the Golden grain,
And those who flung it to the winds like Rain,
  Alike to no such aureate Earth are turn'd
As, buried once, Men want dug up again.

***

Ah, my Beloved, fill the Cup that clears
TO-DAY of past Regrets and future Fears:
  To-morrow--Why, To-morrow I may be
Myself with Yesterday's Sev'n thousand Years.

***

Alike for those who for TO-DAY prepare,
And those that after some TO-MORROW stare,
  A Muezzin from the Tower of Darkness cries,
"Fools! your Reward is neither Here nor There."

***

There was the Door to which I found no Key;
There was the Veil through which I might not see:
  Some little talk awhile of ME and THEE
There was--and then no more of THEE and ME.

***

But if in vain, down on the stubborn floor
Of Earth, and up to Heav'n's unopening Door,
  You gaze TO-DAY, while You are You--how then
TO-MORROW, when You shall be You no more?

***

Waste not your Hour, nor in the vain pursuit
Of This and That endeavor and dispute;
  Better be jocund with the fruitful Grape
Than sadden after none, or bitter, Fruit.

***

I sent my Soul through the Invisible,
Some letter of that After-life to spell:
  And by and by my Soul return'd to me,
And answer'd "I Myself am Heav'n and Hell:"

Gerolamo Cardano (1501-1576)

Girolamo Cardan or Cardano was a celebrated Italian Renaissance mathematician, physician, astrologer and gambler.

Cardano is famed for his work "*Ars Magna*" which was the first Latin treatise devoted solely to algebra. In it he gave the methods of solution of the cubic and quartic equations.

Gerolamo Cardano was the illegitimate child of a lawyer in Milan, Fazio Cardano, and Chiara Micheria. His father has enough knowledge in mathematics, in particular, in geometry: in addition to his law practice, he lectured on geometry at the University of Pavia and Milan.

Being an enthusiast in mathematics, Fazio collected a rich library with ancient books (in particular Euclid, whom Fazio admired). This library and a common atmosphere in the house attracted Leonardo da Vinci, and soon he became a host's friend. It is known that Leonardo with interest read Fazio's book "Tractate on prospective".

When Fazio Cardano was in his fifties, he met Chiara Micheria, who was a young widow with three children. Chiara became pregnant but at that time the plague hit Milan, and before she was due to give birth, she was persuaded to leave the city for nearby Pavia, a small town in Italian province of Lombardy, where Gerolamo was born. Chiara stayed with wealthy Fazio's friends. Here she received news that her other children had died of the plague in Milan.

Chiara lived apart from Fazio for many years though Gerolamo lived at his father home. At that time illegitimate children lived in families with their legitimate siblings and were treated equally. Several years later Fazio did marry Chiara though it did not change Gerolamo's status as illegitimate child.

Gerolamo got his first education from his father taught his son mathematics. He would like his son became his assistant and allowed Gerolamo to enter the Pavia University, where he lectured. However, Gerolamo became a medical student despite his father's wish that he should study law.

At that time a war broke out, the university was closed, so Gerolamo was forced to move to the University of Padua to complete his studies ин 1526.

Shortly after this move, his father died but by this time Cardano already stood on his own foot.

Squandered some money left him by his father, he turned to gambling hoping on fortune. He used to make a living by playing cards, dice and even chess. His understanding of nature of statistics gave him some advantage over his opponents and, on average, he won more than he lost. Gambling became his addiction that took off his time, money and reputation. Gamblers companies are always dubious. Once, when he found that he was cheated playing cards, Cardano even slashed the face of his opponent.

Cardan got his doctorate degree in medicine in 1525 and applied to join the College of Physicians in Milan, where his mother still lived. The College administration did not like him, despite his exceptional abilities: he had a reputation as a difficult man, uncompromising and even aggressive in his opinions defending. However, there should be a legitimate reason for rejection, and it was found: it was discovered that Cardano was illegitimate Fazio's son…

On the advice of a friend of his, Cardano set up a medical practice in a small village 10 miles from Padua. In late 1531 he married a daughter of a captain of the local police. Since medical practice there did not provide enough income for him to support his family, in a year, he moved to another place near Milan. He applied again to the College of Physicians in Milan but again was not allowed membership. Unable to practice medicine, Cardano reverted to gambling to pay his way, but this time fortune was not on his side. Desperately seeking a change of his life, Cardano moved to Milan, but here they fared even worse: the Cardanos had to enter the poorhouse...

At last, Cardano was lucky obtaining Fazio's former post of lecturer in mathematics at the Piatti Foundation. That position gave him plenty of free time and, despite not being a member of the College of Physicians, he treated a few patients to earn decent money for his family. He was so successful, achieving some near miraculous cures that his reputation grew up. He was consulted by members of the College, and his grateful patients and their relatives became whole hearted supporters of Cardano.

Cardano was furious at his continuing exclusion from the College and, in 1536, he published a book attacking the College's medical ability and their Charter. Naturally, when he applied again in 1537, he was again rejected. However, two years later, after much pressure from his influential admirers, the College modified the clause regarding legitimate birth and admitted Cardan.

Since then, Cardano began his prolific literary career writing on a diversity of topics: mathematics, medicine, philosophy, astronomy and theology.

Since 1534 he got a position of mathematics lecturer at the universities of Milan and Bologna though continued his medical practice for financial purposes. In his free time, Cardano compiled horoscopes and interpreted night dreams. Even the Pope of Rome used Cardano's service!

It is interesting that Gerolamo Cardano used a special kind of testing for his method of horoscopes compiling: he created them for dead people whose real lives were well known, for instance, Petrarka[52] and Durer[53].

---

[52] **Francesco Petrarca**, known in English as **Petrarch** (1304-1374) was an Italian scholar, poet, and one of the earliest Renaissance humanists. Petrarch is often popularly called the "father of humanism".

[53] **Albrecht Dürer** (1471-1528) was a German painter and mathematician, one of the greatest master of the Renaissance.

By the way, he unlimitedly trusted in astrology. By legend, he died starving himself to death two days before the date he predicted as a day of his death! Who knows what was the main reason: self-conviction (and Cardano was a kind of an extrasense) or the will to prove his rightwards even by price of life?

He was a superstitious man, believed in miracles and demons, trusted to his presage. He wrote how he foresaw every event happened before his son's execution. He wrote how he guessed sick organs of his patients without examination or saw "the seal of death" on his collocutor's face…

Cardano paid great attention to his own night dreams that he remembered in details and then described in his diary. (By the way, modern psychiatrists even tried to determine Cardano's illnesses by this notes.)

In the end of 1530-s, Cardano began to be interested in solutions of algebraic equations of powers 2 and 3. He met Tartaglia who was known for his knowledge of the solution of cubics, had with him a brief correspondence. There followed a period of intense mathematical study by Cardan who worked on solving cubic and quartic equations by radical over the next six years. In 1545, insert the solution in his famous book "*Ars Magna*" ("*Great Art*"), giving there all credential to Tartaglia. Nevertheless, it led to long and painful process that was described in details above…

In 1540 Cardan resigned from his mathematical position at the Piatti Foundation, leaving his position to his closest pupil and assistant Luigi Ferrari who had brilliantly solved quartic equations by radicals, being inspired by his mentor.

From 1540 to 1542 Cardan abandoned his studies and did nothing but gamble and playing chess all day. He wrote about that time: "I never could express briefly how much damage chess brought to my work…" and "Even more harm was done by playing dice…"

Notice, just for justice, that even those addictions gave some positive "byproduct": he wrote in 1526 book "*Liber de ludo alea*" ("*Book on Games of Chance*") where one can find some knowledge in probability theory , including verbal description of the Law of Large Number (one of the fundamental theorem of the Probability Theory) and some combinatoric problems. (The book was published only in 1563.)

During the years 1543-1552, Cardan lectured on medicine at the University of Pavia and at the Piatti Foundation in Milan, as war frequently forced the closure of the university in Pavia.

In 1546 his wife died on the background of Cardano's fame achieved from his books which were the most readable at that time. He became rector of the College of Physicians and became known as the greatest physician in the world. His fame crossed the borders and he received many offers from the rulers of many European states. However, he only once left Italy: he went (for a substantial sum of money) to Scottish Archbishop who was suffering from asthma for ten years in spite of the court physicians of both the French king and German emperor did their best.

Cardano arrived in Edinburgh in the end of June. By the time he left in September, the Archbishop was already recovering. Within two years the Archbishop let Cardan know that he had made a complete recovery.

Coming back, Cardano was appointed professor of medicine at Pavia University. He became a rich and successful man. But just then Cardano received what he called himself "a crowning misfortune": his eldest son, Giambatista, committed a serious crime.

The story was like in a bad novel. Giambatista secretly married a young woman whose parents were interesting only in "pumping money" from their son-in-law and his rich father. In addition, his wife publicly mocked him for not being the father of their three children.

All this drove Giambatista to poison his wife. He was arrested and he confessed to the crime. Cardano recruited the best lawyers but in vain…In April of 1560, his son was executed…

Cardano was forced to leave the place because he beard the stamp of the father of a convicted murderer and became a hated man himself... He applied for a professorship of medicine at Bologna and was appointed to the post. The time in Bologna was hard for Cardano. Due to his arrogant manner, he created many enemies. After a few years Cardano's colleagues tried to dismiss him, by spreading rumors that his lectures were practically unattended.

In 1570 Cardan was put in jail on the charge of heresy: he had compiled and distributed the horoscope of Jesus Christ. In addition, he wrote a book, in which he praised Nero[54] who historically known tormentor of the martyrs. It seemed strange to those who knew Cardano: he always gave his full support to the church. However, the Great Inquisition was looking to make examples of prominent men whose commitment could be questioned. So, Cardano was chosen...

He spent more than a month in jail but on 43rd day he announced that he began a hunger-strike. (By the way, it was the first political hanger strike in history!) He wrote a letter to Cardinal: "I eat nothing, since eating I became full of anger and furor. Starving myself, I doom myself on death and, consequently, killing my anger". Fortunately, at the moment new Pope of Rome, Gregory XIII mounted to the Throne. He was old Cardano's friend: they were taught together at the University. The Pope claimed that it is reasonable to encourage insurrectionary brains that can reasonably look at the reality". (Evidently, this rule extended only to Pope's friends!)

However, even with such support on his release Cardano had been living until his death under a home surveillance by Inquisition.

Nevertheless, immediately after releasing Cardano went to Rome, where he received an unexpectedly warm reception: he was granted immediate membership of the College of Physicians and the Pope granted him a pension.

At his late years, Cardano had adopted his grandson from his elder son after the death of his daughter-in-law. He inherit ate everything to him after his death.

At the twilight of his life, Cardano wrote book "*De vita propria*" ("*The Book of My Life*") that is considered as one of the best autobiographies. In this book he almost ignored his mathematical research, paying attention only to his medical achievements. He wrote that

---

[54] **Nero Claudius Caesar Augustus Germanicus**[(37-68) was born **Lucius Domitius Ahenobarbus**, and commonly known as **Nero**. He was Roman Emperor from 54 to 68. In 64, most of Rome was destroyed in the Great Fire of Rome. Some historians blamed Nero for this fire. In 68 he was driven from the throne. Facing assassination, he committed suicide. Nero's rule is often associated with tyranny and extravagance. He is known for a number of executions, including those of his mother and stepbrother.

he had described about five thousand types of severe sicknesses and solved about 40 thousand medical problems… (If assume that during his 75-year life he spent 40 years as a medical practitioner, it means that he had healed, on average, about 1000 patients a year). He mentioned that he had only three medical errors in entire his practice. Probably there were some exaggerations though his physician glory was doubtless. He compared himself with such medical genius as Hippocrates[55], Galen[56] and Avicenna.

Cardano wrote: "My will to immortalize my own name appeared very early though I was able to realize that my will too late… Awaiting something from the future, we neglect the present".

The filed of Cardano's scientific interests was extremely wide.

He was one of the first scientists who knowledgeably grounded impossibility of perpetuum mobile creation…

He investigated water steam expansion…

He grounded the theory of sea high and low tides under the Mon and Sun influence…

He first explained the difference between magnetic and electric attractions[57]…

In addition to his major contributions to algebra he also made important contributions to mechanics and geology.

He made the first ever foray into the realm of probability theory that was "terra incognito" at the time.

His book "*De subtilitate rerum*" ("*On Subtlety*") served as a popular textbook on static and hydrostatic during entire XVII century.

Cardano was at the same time an excellent engineer. He invented the Cardan joint a type of universal joint in a shaft that enables it to rotate

[55] **Hippocrates of Cos** (460 – 370 BC) was an ancient Greek physician. He is considered one of the most outstanding figures in the history of medicine. The founder of the Hippocratic school of medicine.

[56] **Galen,** or **Claudius Galenus** (129-200) was a prominent ancient Greek physician, whose theories dominated Western medical science for over a millennium. Wrote over 300 works in philosophy, medicine and pharmacology.

[57] **Thales of Milet** (625 – 545 B.C.) was an ancient Greek philosopher and astronomer, was the first who discovered attraction of a thread by a rubbed amber..

when out of alignment… The story of this invention is rather interesting. When in 1541 Spanish king Carlos V with triumph entered concurred Milan, Gerolamo Cardano, being at the time the Rector of College of Physicians of Milan, was given an honor to walk aside of the king's brougham. As a response for such am honor, he suggested to improve the king's vehicle by a special construction that allowed the brought to keep horizontal position while moving on unflat surface. Now any car has such a pendant that is called "Cardano's pendant".

Being justice, one should mention that analogous attempts had been attempted even in ancient time. And in his "Atlantic Codex" Leonardo da Vinci gave a draft of a ship compass with "Cardano's pendant".

. Cardan also published two encyclopedias of natural science that "... contained a little of everything, from cosmology to the construction of machines, from the usefulness of natural sciences to the evil influence of demons, from the laws of mechanics to cryptology", as wrote one of science historian.

.

Pierre de Fermat
(1601-1655)

French mathematician who made an outstanding input into analytical geometry, the number theory and calculus.

With the name of Fermat, his Great (or Last) Theorem is always associated.

Ideas and discoveries made by Fermat in the number theory dramatically influenced on many generations of mathematicians.

Pierre Fermat was born in Beaumont-de-Lomagne to a wealthy leather merchant and second consul of the city. Pierre had a school education at the local Franciscan monastery. Then he attended the University of Toulouse before moving to Bordeaux in the second half of the 1620s.

He received a degree in civil law and under influence of his father in 1631 became a counselor in the lower chamber of the parliament in Toulouse where he lived the remainder of his life. In 1638 he was appointed to a higher chamber, then in 1652 he was promoted to the highest level at the criminal court.

In 1652 Europe was stricken by the plague. Fermat also was struck down by the illness plague and hardly survived. In 1653 his death was even wrongly reported, then corrected.

Perfectly fulfilling his duties at the parliament, Fermat all his free time was preoccupied with mathematics. Unfortunately he was in some isolation from the French informal mathematical community that was headed by Pascal.

In 1636, one of Fermat colleagues at the parliament moved to Paris as royal librarian and made contact with Mersenne[58] and his group. Mersenne became interested in Fermat's discoveries on falling bodies, and the two began to correspond.

It was somewhat ironical that his initial contact with the scientific community Fermat made through his study of free fall since Fermat actually had little interest in physics. He was much more interested in proving geometrical theorems than in their relation to the real world. Fermat's first letter to Mersenne contained two problems on maxima which Fermat asked Mersenne to pass on to the Paris mathematicians. It was a typical style of Fermat's relations with other mathematicians: he challenged others to find results which he had already obtained.

Probably Fermat did not like to waste time for strong proofs and preferred to jump to a new problem. His colleagues sometimes even blamed him that he was almost teasing them.

Mersenne and Roberval[59] and found that Fermat's problems in this first, and subsequent, letters were extremely difficult and usually not solvable using then known techniques. They asked him to divulge his methods and Fermat sent "*Method for Determining Maxima and Minima and Tangents to Curved Lines*" accompanied with his algebraic approach to geometry to the Paris mathematicians.

His reputation as one of the leading mathematicians in the world came quickly. However, attempts to get his work published failed mainly

[58] **Marin Mersenne** or **le Père Mersenne** (1588 –1648) was a French theologian, philosopher, mathematician and music theorist, often referred to as the "father of acoustics".

[59] **Gilles Personne de Roberval** (1602 - 1675) was a French mathematician. Just before the invention of the infinitesimal calculus, introduced a method involving limits or infinitesimals.

because Fermat never really wanted to put his work into a polished form. For instance, once Pascal, with whom Fermat also began to correspond, literally insisted that the latter had to publish his results, Fermat responded: "In spit of my work could be considered publishable, I don't like to see my name in the publications".

However Fermat soon became engaged in a controversy with Descartes. Mersenne asked him to give an opinion on Descartes' "*La Dioptrique*", which Fermat described as "groping about in the shadows". Fermat claimed that Descartes had not correctly deduced his law of refraction since it was inherent in his assumptions. Descartes was really furious and soon found a reason to feel even angrier since Fermat's work on maxima, minima and tangents was considered as reducing the importance of Descartes' work "*La Géométrie*", which Descartes was most proud. To revenge, Descartes attacked Fermat's method of maxima, minima and tangents. Roberval and Étienne Pascal (Blaise Pascal's father) checked the solution and … the Fermat's correctness was proved! Notice that Descartes admitted Fermat arguments in his writing: "... Seeing the last method that you use for finding tangents to curved lines, I can reply to it in no other way than to say that it is very good".

Nevertheless, Descartes felt offended and tried to damage Fermat's reputation. He wrote to Mersenne claiming that Fermat was inadequate as a mathematician and a thinker. Descartes was important and respected and thus was able to severely damage Fermat's reputation.

Fermat is best remembered for this work in number theory, in particular for Fermat's Last Theorem that we already discussed above.

In 1654 correspondence between Fermat and Blaise Pascal started when the latter, well aware of Fermat's outstanding mathematical abilities, asked him for confirmation about his ideas on probability. Blaise Pascal knew of Fermat through his father, who had died three years before. That short correspondence set up the probability theory and now the two are regarded as joint founders of the subject. Fermat, however, changed the topic from probability to number theory.

In 1656 Fermat had started a correspondence with Huygens. This grew out of Huygens interest in probability and the correspondence was soon manipulated by Fermat onto topics of number theory. However, this topic did not interest Huygens…

Pierre Fermat can be considered as one of the creator of calculus. It is well known that Isaac Newton was a mathematician who first grounded differential calculus and his fought with Gottfried Leibniz for the palm is well known. However, in 1934 there was found a Newton's notice, in which he wrote that developing differential calculus he "based on the Monsieur Fermat's method of tangents to curved lines".

Thus, the role Fermat had played in grounding the probability theory and differential calculus would be enough to give Fermat one of the highest places among mathematicians of the World. And at the same time greatest results in the number theory belonged to him as well.

Blaise Pascal
(1623-1662)

Blaise Pascal is one of the most famous scientists in history.He died when he was just 39-year old but in spit of this he entered the history as an outstanding mathematician, physicist, philosopher and writer.

Blaise Pascal was born in Clermont-Ferrand, in the Auvergne province of France. He lost his mother, Antoinette Begon, when he was only 3-year old. His father, Étienne Pascal was a local judge, who had an interest in science and mathematics.

By the way, well known so-called "Pascal's Snail[60]" belongs namely to Étienne Pascal, not to his famous genius son.

Shortly after the death of his wife, Étienne Pascal moved with his children to Paris. Being a rather educated man himself, he decided to educate his children (he has also two daughters) himself, for they all showed extraordinary intellectual ability. Blaise showed an amazing aptitude for mathematics and science. At the age of eleven, he composed a short treatise on the sounds of vibrating bodies. His father reaction was a bit strange: his son was forbidden to further pursue mathematics until the age of fifteen so as not to harm his study of Latin and Greek.

However, next year Étienne found Blaise writing with a piece of coal on a wall an independent proof that the sum of the angles of a

60 "Pascal's Snail" is a two-dimensional curve that is formed by a point on a circle that id rolling over another circle.

triangle is equal 180^0. Then the father, admired by his son's persistence, changed his mind and permitted his son to study Euclid.

At the age of 14 Blaise started to accompany his father to Père Mersenne's meetings at his monastic cell in Paris that was a frequent meeting place for then famous scientists. Here he was allowed to sit in as a silent on-looker. However, in June 1639, at the age of sixteen, Pascal wrote his first serious work of mathematics "*Essai pour les coniques*" ("*Essay on Conics*") and presented this to one of Mersenne's meetings.

The Pascal's "Hexagram Mysticum Theorem" states that if a hexagon is inscribe in a conic section[61], then the points of intersection of pairs of opposite sides lies on the same line. This not a simple theorem could be illustrated on a rather simple graph.

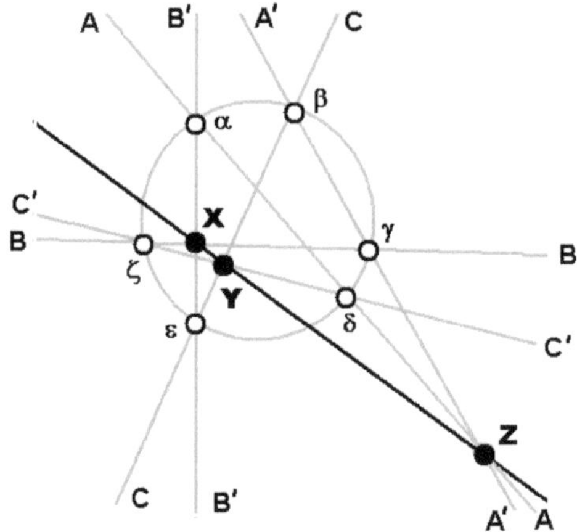

Here circles *α*, *β*, *γ*, *δ*, *ε* and *ζ* denote vertexes of an arbitrary hexagon, and pairs of lines **AA** with **A'A'**, **BB** with **B' B'** and **CC** with **C'C'** form corresponding points of intersection ***X***, ***Y*** and ***Z*** that are lying on a single line.

Pascal's work was so precocious that Descartes, when shown the manuscript, refused to believe that the composition was not by the elder

[61] Curves that form at the intersection of an infinite conic surface and a plane. If the intersection is a closed curve, the section is called an ellipse (of which the circle is a special case). In other cases one has parabolas or hyperbola.

Pascal whom he knew and very much respect. When Mersenne assured him that it was, indeed, done by the young Pascal, Descartes accepted the solution though could not forced himself not to say some unkind words: "I do not find it strange that he has offered demonstrations about conics more appropriate than those of the ancients," adding, "but other matters related to this subject can be proposed that would scarcely occur to a sixteen-year-old child".

Later Pascal presented about 400 colloraries of this theorem…

In 1631 Étienne Pascal left his position, selling his position for good money. (At that time in France positions and offices could be sold and bought.) However, soon he had lost his capital investing it into government's bonds that fall down.

At last in 1639 Étienne Pascal had been appointed the king's commissioner of taxes in Rouen. Here Blaise published his first work – "Essay on Conics".

City tax records were in utter chaos and Étienne had been making exhausting calculations and recalculations of taxes owed and paid. In 1642, trying to help his father in his endless and exhausting job, Blaise, not yet nineteen, constructed a mechanical calculator capable of addition and subtraction. It was called Pascaline. The Pascals decided to produce that machine for selling but was too expensive and failed to be a commercial success: through the next decade only about fifty Pascalinas were built.

In 1646 Étienne Pascal injured his leg and had to recuperate in his house. He was looked after by two young brothers from a religious movement just outside Rouen. They had a profound effect on the young Pascal and he became deeply religious.

By 1646, Pascal had learned of Evangelista Torricelli's[62] experimentation with barometers. Pascal questioned what force kept some mercury in the tube and what filled the space above the mercury in the tube. At Pascal's time a vacuum was impossibility: most scientists, following Aristotle contended that, rather than a vacuum, some invisible matter was present.

[62] **Evangelista Torricelli** (1608–1647) was an Italian physicist and mathematician, best known for his invention of the barometer..

Following more experimentation, in 1647 Pascal wrote "*Experiences nouvelles touchant le vide*" ("*New Experiments with the Vacuum*"), which detailed basic rules describing to what degree various liquids could be supported by air pressure. Thus, Pascal provided the reason why above the column of liquid in a barometer tube it should be indeed a vacuum. It was, probably, one of the most significant works by Pascal though it was published only after his death.

In the fall of 1648, husband of Pascal's elder sister, trying to confirm the Pascal's theory had performed an experiment: under surveillance of several witnesses: he measured air pressure on the valley and then on the top of a hill.

He wrote to his brother-in-law: "First I poured sixteen pounds of quicksilver (i.e. mercury) in to a vessel, then took several glass tubes, each four feet long and hermetically sealed at one end and opened at the other. Then placed them in the vessel and found that the quicksilver stood at 26" and 3½ lines above the quicksilver in the vessel. Taking the other tube and a portion of the quicksilver, I walked to the top of Puy-de-Dôme[63] , about 500 fathoms[64] higher than the monastery, and found that the quicksilver reached a height of only 23" and 2 lines[65]...I repeated the experiment five times with care...each at different points on the summit".

However, Pascal's insistence on the existence of the vacuum led to conflict with a number of other prominent scientists, including Descartes who met with Pascal and had with him two day embittered discussion. Afterwards Descartes wrote, rather cruelly, in a letter to Huygens[66] that Pascal "*...has too much vacuum in his head*".

Next year Pascal replicated the experiment fulfilled by his brother-in-law. He carried a barometer up to the top of a bell tower at the church

[63] **Puy-de-Dôme is** a mountain that in the pre-Christian time served as an assembly place for spiritual ceremonies. By coincidence, the temple located there was dedicated to the God Mercury!

[64] **A fathom** is a unit of length with the size varies from system to system. The international fathom equals 2 yards.

[65] **Line** equals 1/12 of inch.

[66] **Christiaan Huygens** (1629–1695) was a prominent Dutch mathematician, astronomer, physicist and horologist.

of Saint-Jacques-de-la-Boucherie, a height of about fifty meters. The mercury height dropped two lines. These experiments carried out by Pascal, were hailed throughout Europe: the barometer was recognized as an instrument!

This time Descartes wrote to one of his friends: "*It was I who advised him to do such experiment though I somehow did not perform it myself. I was sure that Pascal was right...*» So, literally in half a year Descartes transformed from Pascal's rival to Pascal's supporter! (It once more confirms a proverb that a success has a many parents when a failure is always an orphan...)

These experiments led Pascal to new practical inventions: he invented hydraulic press and syringe. Of course, construction of barometer itself was improved.

From as early as his eighteenth year, Pascal suffered from a nervous ailment with a terrible pain. In 1647, a paralytic attack and he was so disabled that could not move without crutches. He moved with his sister to Paris and under surveillance of excellent physician his health improved, but his nervous system had been permanently damaged: he deepened into hypochondria, which affected his character and his philosophy.

In addition, in 1651 his father, whom he loved and deified, died. Blaise fell down in a deep depression. Nothing is known about next three years of his life, though it is said that during this period he wrote his "*Discours sur les passions de l'amour*" ("*Discourses on the Passion of Love*").

Renewing his health, he again started to work. Pascal's work in the fields of the study of hydrodynamics and hydrostatics centered on the principles of hydraulic fluids. He wrote "*Treatise on the Equilibrium of Liquids*", in which he explains law of pressure that now bears his name. This treatise is a complete outline of a system of hydrostatics, the first in the history of science, it embodied his most distinctive and important contribution to physical theory.

As most of his great contemporaries, he confirmed his theoretical approaches with practical applications. He invented the hydraulic press (using hydraulic pressure to multiply force) and the syringe.

In 1653, Blaise Pascal wrote his "*Traité du triangle arithmétique*" ("*Treatise on the Arithmetical Triangle*") in which he described a convenient tabular presentation for binomial coefficients (now called "Pascal's triangle").

In 1654, prompted by a friend interested in gambling problems, he corresponded with Fermat on the subject, and from that collaboration was born the mathematical theory of probabilities.

In spite of his bad health, Pascal continued scientific research. In a letter to Fermat he wrote: "… though I am still chained to a bed, I can inform you that yesterday I got your letter and working on my answer to you".

In November of 1654, Pascal had been involved in an accident over a bridge above the river Seine: the horses plunged over the parapet and the carriage nearly followed them. Fortunately, the reins broke and the coach hung halfway over the edge. Pascal and his friends emerged unharmed, but terrified Pascal fainted away and remained unconscious for some time. Upon recovering, Pascal once had a religious vision: he met with God and Jesus Christ. Awaking, he immediately recorded the experience in a brief note to himself. It was concluded by quoting one of Psalms: "I will not forget thy word. Amen". Later he sewn this document into his coat and always transferred it when he changed clothes. It was discovered by his servant after his death.

After a religious experience in 1654, Pascal mostly gave up work in mathematics. He visited monasteries, avoided people. He became weak, his skin was yellow. "I am so weak that cannot walk without a stick and afraid to ride horses…" – wrote he to Fermat.

However, once in 1658, after a sleepless night, he anonymously offered a prize for the quadrature of a cycloid. Solutions were offered by several scientists, among which was Huygens. Pascal, under a pseudonym, published his own solution, which has been already obtained by him before the starting the competition. (By the way, some results from here were used by Leibniz for developing of the differential calculus.) Controversy and heated argument followed after Pascal announced himself the winner.

Maybe it was a joke-to-depart of genius?

His belief and religious commitment revitalized, he began to pray and study the Bible. At that moment his priest was attacked by Jesuits and even his dossier had been sent to the Archbishop. Defending his friend

Pascal wrote "*Lettres provincials*" ("*The Provincial Letters*") and published it anonymously. This work pretended to be the report of a Parisian to a friend in the provinces on the moral and theological issues. The 18-letter series was published in Cologne between 1656 and 1657 under the pseudonym Louis de Montalte. It is considered now that Pascal reached a new level of style in French prose. This book infuriated King of France Louis XIV who ordered to burn it in 1660.

Aside from their religious influence, the Provincial Letters were popular as a literary work. Pascal's humor and vicious satire influenced the prose of later French writers like Voltaire[67] and Jean-Jacques Rousseau[68]. Voltaire called the Letters "the best-written book that has yet appeared in France".

Pascal became more and more religious. He visited one church after another, he gave his belongings to poor people… He beard a chlamys with nails and when a "wrong thought" visited his head, he hit himself and nails cut his body…

Pascal made himself an armorial emblem of an eye surrounded by a crown of thorns. There were inscripted words: "Scio cui credidi" ("I know whom I have believed"). His beliefs renewed, he set his mind to write his testament, the "*Pensées*" ("*Thoughts*"), his most influential theological work, that he could not finish. In this work Pascal surveyed several philosophical paradoxes: infinity and nothing, faith and reason, soul and matter, death and life, meaning and vanity…

This work contains the so-called "Pascal's wager", which claims to prove that belief in God is rational with the following argument:

Belief is a wise wager. Granted that faith cannot be proved, what harm will come to you if you gamble on its truth and it proves false? If you gain, you gain all; if you lose, you lose nothing. Wager, then, without hesitation, that He exists.

Blaise Pascal died when he was only 39 year old…

*****

---

[67] **François-Marie Arouet**, pen name **Voltaire** (1694 - 1778), was a French Enlightenment writer, essayist, deist and philosopher.

[68] **Jean-Jacques Rousseau** (1712 –1778) was a Genevan philosopher whose political ideas influenced the French Revolution.

Pascal's works cover various fields of human knowledge. Beside a number of his achievements, which have been already mentioned above, there are some popular everyday used inventions whose creator name is unknown. Thus, nowadays, hardly a percent of the people know that an ordinary wheelbarrow has been invented by Blaise Pascal. He also suggested an idea of omnibus: a popular coach with fixed marchroute – that is the first type of popular transportation.

In honor of his scientific contributions, the name Pascal has been given to the SI unit of pressure, to a programming language, and Pascal's law (an important principle of hydrostatics), and as mentioned above, Pascal's triangle and Pascal's wager still bear his name.

In literature, Pascal is regarded as one of the most important authors of the French Classical Period and is read today as one of the greatest masters of French prose. His use of satire and wit influenced later polemicists.

Quotations by Blaise Pascal

- All of our reasoning ends in surrender to feeling.
- Atheism shows strength of mind, but only to a certain degree.
- Can anything be stupider than that a man has the right to kill me because he lives on the other side of a river and his ruler has a quarrel with mine, though I have not quarrelled with him?
- Contradiction is not a sign of falsity, nor the lack of contradiction a sign of truth.
- Do you wish people to think well of you? Don't speak well of yourself.
- Earnestness is enthusiasm tempered by reason.
- Eloquence is a painting of the thoughts.
- Evil is easy, and has infinite forms.
- Few friendships would survive if each one knew what his friend says of him behind his back.
- I cannot judge my work while I am doing it. I have to do as painters do, stand back and view it from a distance, but not too great a distance.

- If our condition were truly happy, we would not seek diversion from it in order to make ourselves happy.
- Imagination decides everything.
- In each action we must look beyond the action at our past, present, and future state, and at others whom it affects, and see the relations of all those things. And then we shall be very cautious.
- It is natural for the mind to believe and for the will to love; so that, for want of true objects, they must attach themselves to false.
- It is not certain that everything is uncertain.
- It is not good to be too free. It is not good to have everything one wants.
- Justice and power must be brought together, so that whatever is just may be powerful, and whatever is powerful may be just.
- Justice and truth are too such subtle points that our tools are too blunt to touch them accurately.
- Justice without force is powerless; force without justice is tyrannical.
- Kind words do not cost much. Yet they accomplish much.
- Little things console us because little things afflict us.
- Love has reasons which reason cannot understand.
- Man's greatness lies in his power of thought.
- Our nature consists in movement; absolute rest is death.
- The charm of fame is so great that we like every object to which it is attached, even death.
- The greater intellect one has, the more originality one finds in men. Ordinary persons find no difference between men.
- The knowledge of God is very far from the love of Him.
- The last thing one knows when writing a book is what to put first.
- The least movement is of importance to all nature. The entire ocean is affected by a pebble.
- The more I see of men, the better I like my dog.
- The only shame is to have none.

- The present letter is a very long one, simply because I had no patience to make it shorter.
- The sensitivity of men to small matters, and their indifference to great ones, indicates a strange inversion.
- The struggle alone pleases us, not the victory.
- The supreme function of reason is to show man that some things are beyond reason.
- There are only two kinds of men: the righteous who think they are sinners and the sinners who think they are righteous.
- There are two types of mind ... the mathematical, and what might be called the intuitive. The former arrives at its views slowly, but they are firm and rigid; the latter is endowed with greater flexibility and applies it simultaneously to the diverse lovable parts of that which it loves.
- Time heals griefs and quarrels, for we change and are no longer the same persons. Neither the offender nor the offended are any more themselves.
- To have no time for philosophy is to be a true philosopher.
- Too much and too little wine. Give him none, he cannot find truth; give him too much, the same.
- Two things control men's nature, instinct and experience.
- We are usually convinced more easily by reasons we have found ourselves than by those which have occurred to others.
- We know the truth, not only by the reason, but also by the heart.
- We never love a person, but only qualities.
- We only consult the ear because the heart is wanting.
- We run carelessly to the precipice, after we have put something before us to prevent us seeing it.
- When we are in love we seem to ourselves quite different from what we were before.
- Words differently arranged have a different meaning, and meanings differently arranged have different effects.
- You always admire what you really don't understand.

Evariste Galois (1811-1832)

French mathematician famous for his contributions to the part of higher algebra now known as group theory. His theory provided a solution to the long-standing question of determining when an algebraic equation can be solved by radicals

Evaristee Galois was born in 1811 in Bourg-la-Reine, a small town near Paris that today became a close suburb of the French capital.

His father, Nicolas Nicolas-Gabriel Galois was a mayor of the town. He was a Republican and was head of local section of liberal party.

He was an intelligent man, knowledgeable and known for his poetry.

At the age of ten he was sent to a college in Reims though very son his mother decided that Evariste was too small and defenseless to be sent off so far from home. He was allowed to stay home, enjoy the quiet family live and his mother, an educated woman, became a sole source of education. He received an excellent education in Latin, Greek and rhetoric.

At the age of twelve, Evariste entered the Lycée of Louis-le-Grand[69] in Paris, which was his first school. Due to his home education he was accepted at the third-year class.

The turbulent political events of the time – struggle between church, royalists and republicans – influenced as well on the school atmosphere: a rapid change of headmasters, rebellion of pupils (about 40 of them were expelled from the school). However, Evariste being a freshman was not involved in any political activity: he spent his time for hard study.

At first Galois did well in school and won prizes, but by his second year he became bored with the classical studies. The headmaster of the school advised his father to let his son repeat the class, because he didn't seem mature for the last class.

His work became mediocre, and he had trouble with the school authorities.

In February 1827 Galois, being 16-year old enrolled in his first mathematics class. Galois worked with Legendre's[70] text on geometry (a rather difficult book!) and quickly mastered it. The algebra textbook, used in the school, disgusted him. At the age of 15, he was reading the original papers of Lagrange[71] and Abel[72], work intended for professional mathematicians!

---

[69] **The Lycée Louis-le-Grand** is a public high school located in Paris, widely regarded as one of the best in France. The school was named in honor of king Louis XIV of France after he visited the school and offered his patronage.

[70] **Adrien-Marie Legendre** (1752 - 1833) was a French mathematician. He made important contributions to statistics, number theory, abstract algebra and mathematical analysis.

[71] **Joseph-Louis, comte de Lagrange** (1736 -1813) was an Italian-French mathematician and astronomer who made important contributions to all fields of analysis and number theory and to classical and celestial mechanics. Considered as one of the greatest mathematicians of the 18th century.

[72] **Niels Henrik Abel** (1802-1829) was a Norwegian mathematician who accomplished

At the same time he neglected other courses. His teachers complained that he didn't participate in lessons and hardly did any homework. They described him as “not wicked”, “original and queer”, “argumentative”. One of them wrote in the school report:

> *“What's dominating him is the fury of mathematics. I think that it would be better for him if his parents would agree to let him study solely mathematics. He is wasting his time here and he does nothing but torments his teachers and get into trouble”.*

His attitude did not change when he is finally admitted to the final class. Probably there, Galois was first time interested in politics.

Galois wanted to go to the École Polytechnique in Paris under all conditions, because it guaranteed him the best possibilities in mathematics. By that time, the École had drastically modified their statutes: no more military orientation, uniforms had been changed for civilian clothes. Fortunately, the major task remained the same: to train young scientists for the state.

In June 1928 Evariste appeared there for the entrance examination, although he had not taken part in another special course in mathematics for another year. He flunked the exam…

In the beginning of the year 1829 in Bourg-la-Reine a young priest took over the parish and soon banded together with the Ultras. Together with a member of the town council he intrigued against the liberal mayor Nicolas Nicolas-Gabriel Galois. They spread falsified vulgar poems and put Nicolas' as the author. Due to the scandal, Evariste's father quitted his mayor position and moved to Paris. Soon he was found dead: he committed suicide on the July 2nd. He hanged himself in his Paris apartment only a few steps from Louis-le-Grand where his son was studying. Galois was deeply affected by his father's death and it greatly influenced entire his life.

His funeral in Bourg-la-Reine became a triumphal procession of the liberals. During the procession, stones were thrown at the priest who hypocritically attended the funeral.

---

an amazing amount of brilliant work in his short lifetime.

Just a few days after the unexpected death of his father, Galois took the entrance examination to the École Polytechnique for the second time. He understood that this time a refusal would be final, if he would flunk again.

This Galois' exam became a legend in the history of mathematics. One of the two examiners asked the question about the theory of the "arithmetic logarithms". Galois criticized immediately the question, mentioning to a professor that there were no "arithmetic logarithms", there were logarithms. Thereupon Galois refused to explain some propositions concerning logarithms, saying that answers were completely obvious!

The examiners were not capable of detecting the mathematical genius of Evariste Galois. They only felt offended by a youth who showed the two professors their ignorance.

Galois, solving problems completely in his head, did not use the chalk and the sponge, just keeping them in his hands. One of the examiners stubbornly continued to ask him incorrect questions. In a fury and despair Galois hurled the sponge into the face of his tormentor…

Years later Terquem[73] remarked, "A candidate of superior intelligence is lost with an examiner of inferior intelligence".

Having been denied admission to Polytechnique, Galois took the Baccalaureate examinations in order to enter the Ecole Normale[74], a far inferior institution for mathematical studies. Here some professors sympathetic to him. His examiner in mathematics reported: "This pupil is sometimes obscure in expressing his ideas, but he is intelligent and shows a remarkable spirit of research".

In the following year, Galois published his first paper on continued fractions. It was at around the same time when he began making fundamental discoveries in the theory of polynomial equations, and he submitted two papers on this topic to the Academy of Sciences. Cauchy[75] refereed these papers, but refused to accept them for publication

---

[73] **Olry Terquem** (1782 -1862) was a French mathematician, best known for his work in geometry. He was among the first who recognized the importance of the work of Évariste Galois.

[74] The **École normale supérieure** is a prestigious French high school.

[75] **Augustine Louis Cauchy** (1789 - 1857) was a French mathematician. His writings

for reasons that still remain unclear. It appears that Cauchy had recognized the importance of Galois' work, though recommended young man to combine the two manuscripts into a single, more comprehensive paper.

The students of the Ecole Normale were set on fire by the events of the July revolution. The director of the school wanted to prevent his students from taking part in the dangerous events on the Paris streets. He ordered students to stay inside the building and had all gates locked.

Galois wanted to take part in actions and tried to escape by climbing over the outer walls. He failed, bruising his hands and knees though fled fro the school.

After the July events, Galois joined the "Société des Amis du Peuple" ("Society of Friends of the People), a most active and aggressive organization of the republican party. They worked as a secret organization and were regarded as very dangerous by most of the press.

Galois seems to have been in continuous conflict with the Society's leaders: he wanted to introduce uniforms (like the one at the Ecole Polytechnique), asked for the students to be armed, so they could have military training. Most of his fellow students were avoiding Galois and his radical ideas.

Evariste was expelled from the school because he was claimed the author of an anonymous letter to the "Gazette des écoles". In this letter the director was blamed and offended for his behavior during the July revolution. Galois never admitted being the author of this letter neither to his fellow students nor to the director.

Even before his expulsion from Ecole Normale, Galois enlisted in the Artillery unit of the National Guard, almost entirely consisting of republicans.

In December 1830, king Louis-Philippe dismissed General Lafayette[76] and disbanded the National Guard out of fear that they might destabilize his government. So it was, that in January 1831 Galois, no longer a student, and not a member of he National Guard anymore.

cover the entire range of mathematics and mathematical physics.

[76] **Marie-Joseph-Paul-Yves-Roch-Gilbert du Motier, Marquis de Lafayette** (1757 - 1834) was a French military officer and former aristocrat who participated in both the American and French revolutions.

His mother was not capable to support him financially, so Evariste tried to found a private algebra class to earn money for his living. His course was attended by about 40 students, mainly friends and not mathematicians. Nobody can explain how Galois could keep them at his abstract lectures!

At age 19, Galois wrote three original papers on the theory of algebraic equations. He submitted them to the Academy of Sciences for the Grand Prix of the Academy in mathematics. The Secretary of the Academy at the time was Fourier[77]. He took them home to read, but then died before writing a report about them and the papers were never found. . With support from Jacques Sturm, Galois published three papers in April 1830. However, he learnt in June that the prize of the Academy would be awarded the Prize jointly to Abel[78] (posthumously) and to Jacobi[79], his own work never having been considered.

Galois was invited by Poisson to submit a third version of his memoir on equation to the Academy and he did so on 17 January 1831.

At around that time, nineteen artillery officers were arrested and charged with conspiracy to overthrow the government because they refused to hand over their arms. The trial of them caused a lot of attention in Paris, so the government, being afraid of an unpopular sentence, ended with an acquittal for the whole group. The members of the Société des Amis du Peuple organized a banquet in honor of the artillerymen, which was held in May. Evariste Galois was among guests.

Alexander Dumas[80], who was one of the guests, wrote in his memoirs: "It would be difficult to find in all Paris, two hundred persons more hostile to the government than those to be found reunited at five

---

77 **Jean Baptiste Joseph Fourier** (1768 -1830) was a French mathematician and physicist. He is best known for investigation of the Fourier series and the Fourier transform named in his honor.

78 **Niels Henrik Abel** (1802 -1829) was a Norwegian mathematician. Proved the impossibility of solving algebraically the general equation of the fifth degree.

79 **Carl Gustav Jacob Jacobi** (1804 - 1851), German mathematician, widely considered as the most inspiring teacher of his time. Jacobian matrix is called in his honor.

80 **Alexandre Dumas** ("father"), born **Dumas Davy de la Pailleterie** (1802 - 1870) was a French writer, best known for his numerous historical novels (The Count of Monte Cristo, The Three Musketeers, The Man in the Iron Mask, and others).

o'clock in the afternoon in the long hall on the ground floor above the garden".

The gathered men did not intend to provoke the police with the toasts, some guests couldn't restrain from flamboyant republican speeches. However, the Galois' "toast" immediately led to chaos and an untimely end of the event. He had raised a knife and exclaimed: "To Louis-Philippe!" Come others followed his example, and immediately panic began: most people afraid of the police coming left the room in a hurry, some of them even through the open windows into the garden.

The next day, the police arrested Galois at his mother apartment with whom he lived. He was charged and imprisoned. On the June 15th he was tried for threatening the King's life.

His lawyer worked out the following strategy of defense: people presumably didn't hear all of his words due to the din in the room. "To Louis-Philippe, if he betrays us!" was what he said, while accidentally brandishing the knife with which he was cutting his meat during the meal. After a long trial the verdict was not guilty.

Just a month after his acquittal, Galois ran into trouble again. The republicans organized a patriotic demonstration for the celebrations of the July 14th at the Place de la Bastille. They wanted to plant a symbolic tree of liberty. The police wanted to prevent the event and broke into suspects' houses (including Galois) during the night preceding the Bastille Day. Galois had been warned by friends and was not home, but the following day he was preventatively arrested together with his friend. He was dressed in uniform of the disbanded artillery, which was strictly forbidden, and in addition was armed to the teeth, carrying besides his usual knife, several pistols.

For this, he was again arrested, this time sentenced to six months in prison for illegally wearing a uniform. He was released on April 29,

1832. During his imprisonment, he continued developing his mathematical ideas.

This time after three months of preventive detention, Galois was harshly punished to nine month in prison until April 1832.

When Galois' prison term went to expiration, one of the worst world-wide raging cholera epidemics had arrived in France and was taking the lives of many people all over France. The prisoners of the jail, where

Galois was incarcerated, were also in jeopardy, so the officials decided to transfer the youngest and those in bad health to a clinic.

While in prison he received a rejection of his memoir. Poisson had reported:

> *"His (Galois') argument is neither sufficiently clear nor sufficiently developed to allow us to judge its rigor".*

However, the Poisson's rejection report ends on an encouraging note: "We would then suggest that the author should publish the whole of his work in order to form a definitive opinion". It was unsurprising, in the light of his character and situation at the time, that Galois reacted violently to the rejection letter. He decided to publish his papers privately through his friend Auguste Chevalier instead of trying to it through the Academy. Apparently, however, Galois did not ignore Poisson's advice and began collecting all his mathematical manuscripts while he was still in prison, and continued polishing his ideas until he was finally released from the jail.

While being in prison, Galois attempted to commit suicide by stabbing himself with a dagger but the other prisoners prevented him. Later he poured out his soul to one of his friends:

> *"Do you know what I lack my friend? I confide it only to you: it is someone whom I can love and love only in spirit. I have lost my father and no one has ever replaced him..."*

In March 1832 a cholera epidemic swept Paris and prisoners, including Galois, were transferred to a hospital. There he apparently fell in love with Stephanie, the daughter of the resident physician. After he was released, Galois exchanged letters with Stephanie, and it is clear that she tried to distance herself from the affair.

Probably, her refusal was one of the main reasons for Evariste's tragic death that happened under the following circumstances. A few days later Galois encountered some of his political enemies and "an affair of honor" (a duel) was arranged. The motive of this Galois' challenge kept unknown but there were hints that it was linked with Stephanie.

Galois knew he had little chance in the duel, so he spent all night writing the mathematics which he didn't want to die with him, often writing “I have no time”, “I have no time” in the margins. He sent these results as well as the ones the Academy had lost to his friend Auguste Chevalier, and, on May 30, 1832, went out to duel with pistols at 25 paces.

The duel and the events leading to it are blurred by time. However, a bright Galois personality literally forced novelists and biographers to invent realistic and non-realistic legends. One of the most popular legends is that the duel was a plot of the royalists to murder him. Probably it was Galois himself who incited this interpretation. He dropped several remarks pointing in this direction at that banquet in honor of the artillerymen as well as his last letters.

However, one should not exclude a much more trivial reason: he was weary of life due to his unhappy love affair, his fruitless efforts for gaining recognition for his mathematical work, his financial and work situation and loss of political platform… So his duel, probably, was like just a staged suicide.

Galois was shot in the intestines, and was taken to the hospital. There he comforted his brother, during the latter visit to his bed, with the words: “Don't cry, I need all my courage to die at twenty”.

He died the day after the duel and was buried in an unmarked, common grave.

Galois' brother and his friend Auguste Chevalier copied his mathematical papers and sent them to Gauss, Jacobi and others. It had been Galois' wish that Jacobi and Gauss should give their opinions on his work. No record exists of any comment these men made. However the papers reached Liouville[81] who, in September 1843, announced to the Academy that he had found in Galois' papers a concise solution:

[81] **Joseph Liouville** (1809 - 1882) was a French mathematician, best known for his work on the existence of a transcendental number. Developed differential equations called now Sturm-Liouville.

> *...as correct as it is deep of this lovely problem: given an irreducible equation of prime degree, decide whether or not it is soluble by radicals.*

He finished his comments with a glowing commentary:

> *I experienced an intense pleasure at the moment when, having filled in some slight gaps, I saw the complete correctness of the method by which Galois proves.*

Liouville published these papers of Galois in his Journal in 1846.

The theory that Galois outlined in these papers is now called Galois theory.

Galois' complete works fill only 60 pages! However, he is considered as one of the most influential mathematician of modern time.

Self-advertising page

You can buy the following my books of series "Legends and Stories about mathematical Insights" in English:

These books can be found at http://www.lulu.com/shop/ in search window choose "BOOK", then in the next window type "USHAKOV". Make your choice!

At the same site you can find another my books.

www.ingramcontent.com/pod-product-compliance
Ingram Content Group UK Ltd.
Pitfield, Milton Keynes, MK11 3LW, UK
UKHW041926190726
13854UKWH00003B/1463